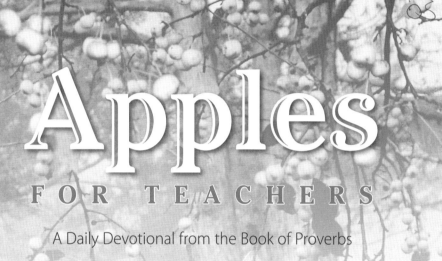

Apples
FOR TEACHERS

A Daily Devotional from the Book of Proverbs

BY FRANK HAMRICK

PositiveAction
FOR CHRIST

Apples for Teachers: A Daily Devotional from the Book of Proverbs

Copyright © 2002, 2008 by Positive Action For Christ, Inc. P.O. Box 700, 502 W. Pippen Street, Whitakers, NC 27891-0700. All rights reserved. No part may be reproduced in any manner without permission in writing from the publisher.

Third printing 2008.

Printed in the United States of America

ISBN: 978-1-929784-90-5

Edited by C.J. Harris

Layout and Design by Shannon Brown

Published by

Preface

This book contains thoughts from the book of Proverbs that are an outgrowth of my personal devotional life. My goal in writing this was really quite simple—to communicate a philosophy of Christian education that is more concerned with the heart than with the head. Academics are important, but the real key to Christian education is reaching the hearts of your students and giving them a passion for God.

Hopefully these thoughts will minister to your soul and be "an ornament of grace and chains about thy neck" (Prov. 1:9) to enhance your ministry. My prayer is that this book will be a daily reminder to you about what's truly important.

Frank Hamrick
Rocky Mount, North Carolina

Apple 1

PROVERBS 1:1
"The proverbs of Solomon the son of David, king of Israel."

Pithy Proverbs

The wisest human who ever lived spoke in proverbs. Solomon understood that terse, pithy statements stick. We are often too verbose, and thus, less memorable. As teachers, our desire should be to make what we say memorable. This was Solomon's concern. He took profound truth and reduced it to easily understood phrases. He used comparisons, similes, and word pictures ("apples of gold in pictures of silver"). Why? He wanted youth not just to hear, but also to understand, apply, and remember. The wise teacher of our day does the same.

Good teachers do not drone. They are not like a saw that rasps against the grain eight hours a day. Rather, they are like jackhammers, impacting kids with exciting, memorable bursts. Choose which of the following is easier to remember and understand:

"Good enough is never good enough."

"Kids, don't be mediocre. You always need to do your very best."

Learn to be pithy, precise, and picturesque in your teaching. Wise teachers do! Ask God to give you the creativity to make your subjects understandable, practical, and memorable today.

Final thought: Use your words to grab your students' attention and focus it on God.

Knowledge Versus Wisdom

Teachers impart knowledge. Good teachers impart wisdom. It is good for our students to know 2+2=4. It is better that our students know that behind the strict mathematical code is a God of order, organization, detail, and exactness.

The purpose of Proverbs is to teach wisdom. What is wisdom? Some have said it is the practical application of knowledge, but I don't think that definition goes far enough.

James 3:15–17 describes two kinds of wisdom: earthly wisdom and wisdom from above. Earthly wisdom may be the practical application of knowledge, but people go to hell if they only have earthly wisdom. A builder may use mathematical measurements to build a house wisely, but that doesn't mean he is wise.

Heavenly wisdom is more than the practice of knowledge. This wisdom is "from above." That is, it finds its home in the Godhead. Colossians tells us that in Christ "are hid all the treasures of wisdom and knowledge" (Col. 2:3). In Colossians 1:9–10 Paul prays that we would be filled "in all wisdom and spiritual understanding…in the knowledge of God."

True wisdom is teaching our students to know and love the Lord. The wise teacher consciously reveals God in every discipline: in mathematical formulas, in historical events, in geographical features, in all the sciences, and, yes, in language.

When our students see the *Lord* in our teaching, rather than the *facts* of our teaching, we impart wisdom.

Final thought: Are we just teachers, or are we wise teachers?

Apple 3

PROVERBS 1:3

"To receive the instruction of wisdom, justice, and judgment, and equity."

Great Goals 1

Here are four great personal goals for a wise teacher: wisdom, justice, judgment, and equity. Today we will discuss the first goal.

We must not merely instruct in wisdom, we must ourselves *receive* the instruction of wisdom. *Receive* is the translation of a Hebrew word that means "to accept, to believe, to commit to." The concept of possession is inherent in the meaning of this word. Thus, a wise teacher must be personally saturated with wisdom. Wise teachers are literally dripping with the knowledge of God in their daily lives. Wise teachers are totally committed to knowing, loving, and enjoying the Lord. Is this your goal? Do you daily seek fellowship with Him? Does your heart pant for God (Ps. 42:1)?

Proverbs 1:2–4 describes the wise teacher. A wise teacher knows the Lord (experiential fellowship, v. 2) and is possessed by this knowledge (v. 3). Like Paul, he counts all things but loss "for the excellency of the knowledge of Christ Jesus my Lord." Ask God to give you a thirst for Him that can only be satisfied (as David puts it) when "I remember thee upon my bed, and meditate on thee in the night watches" (Ps. 63:5–6). When this is your quest, your pursuit, and the longing of your soul, your students will soon take note. Be a receptive (possessed) teacher today.

Final thought: The wise teacher knows God and desires to share that relationship with her students.

Great Goals 2

Here are the four goals of wise teachers: to be possessed by wisdom, justice, judgment, and equity. Today we look at the second of these goals.

We must be possessed by justice. *Justice* is the Hebrew word most often translated "righteousness," and most often refers not only to the quality of righteousness but also to right living. Experiential knowledge of God leads to righteous living.

Teachers sometimes mistakenly demand righteousness from their students. True biblical righteousness, however, comes from the inside. As we know and love Him, our lives ooze with His righteousness. Personal, intimate fellowship with the Lord produces an inner pressure that forces righteous living into our lives. The same is true of our students.

Your mission today is to instill this passion for God that works out righteousness in your students. Righteousness is not mandated or molded—it is pressed out from within! Be on guard against externally molding your students to do right. Rather, ask God to help you exude such a love for Him that your students are caught up in that same love. You will soon see the "oozing" of righteousness in their lives.

Final thought: Remember that true righteousness must always grow from the inside out.

Apple 5

PROVERBS 1:3

"To receive the instruction of wisdom, justice, and judgment, and equity."

Great Goals 3 & 4

Previously we have discussed two of the four goals of a Christian teacher for her own life. Today we see the final two goals: to be possessed by judgment and equity.

Godly teachers are possessed by good judgment. The Hebrew here refers to decision–making. Its biblical usage is especially applied to leaders. Wise teachers make wise decisions. But where do they get that wisdom? When our knowledge of and love for the Lord possesses our souls, we make wise decisions. Salvation alone does not guarantee wise choices. Only knowledge of Him guarantees such.

But we must also be possessed by equity. The Hebrew word is an interesting one. It simply means "ease, level, smooth." It gradually came to stand for the easy-going spirit of a person that causes her to be at peace with those around her. *Level* carries the concept of honesty and trustworthiness. These two ideas convey equity. The teacher, through developing a passionate love for and knowledge of the Lord, is at peace with her class and fellow teachers. One who enjoys God enjoys her students. One who is at peace with God is at peace with her students. Do your students love to be around you? Do they seek you out at ballgames or in the mall?

Final thought: Ask God to give you peace with your students and to destroy any adversarial spirit you may have.

"To give subtlety to the simple, to the young man knowledge and discretion."

Goals for Teaching

What should be the teacher's goal for his own teaching? The objective is "to give subtlety…knowledge and discretion." Note the progression of verbs in Proverbs 1:2–4. First, we must have an intimate knowledge (experiential knowledge) of the Lord (true wisdom). Second, we must understand the implications of that wisdom. Third, we must be possessed by that wisdom. Finally, we must give that same wisdom to our students.

Until we fully grasp True Wisdom, we have nothing to give our students. We can dispense academic information, but until we are saturated with Him, we cannot transfer wisdom.

Give is a translation of the Hebrew word meaning "to practice, teach, or share." We can only share what we have experienced. True teaching is far more than dispensing information. A teacher is a sharer of his own experiences. Jesus shared His life and His heart with his disciples. They became learners of Him.

Notice the subjects of this sharing. The word "simple" means those who through lack of experience do not yet fully comprehend or understand. We often accuse youth of ungodliness, when in reality they only lack maturity. We sometimes misinterpret immaturity as rebellion. It takes patience to share with the inexperienced and the immature. This kind of patience only comes when verses 2–3 are true in our lives. Do you have the patience and the honesty to share your heart and experiences (failures and triumphs) in your daily walk? This alone will give "subtlety to the inexperienced" and "knowledge and discretion" to the young.

Final thought: Share today one failure and one triumph in your walk with the Lord with your students.

Apple 7

PROVERBS 1:5

"A wise man will hear, and will increase learning: and a man of understanding shall attain unto wise counsels."

Producing Helmsmen

This verse points us to the kind of students our schools must produce. Let's work backwards in this verse. The ultimate goal of a Christian school (and teacher) is to produce students who "attain unto wise counsels." Literally, the phrase *wise counsels* can be translated "helmsman" (one who steers a ship). Thus, our schools are naval academies producing young men and women capable of steering their own lives and the lives of others. Are our graduates equipped to steer their lives in a godly direction on an ungodly sea? Are our seniors steering the lower classmen in a godly direction?

Back up one phrase to "a man of understanding." Helmsmen understand. They perceive the wisdom of God. They love Him and experience fellowship with Him daily. Is this true of the seniors in your school? What about your class? Are you consciously teaching them how to counsel themselves so they can counsel others biblically?

Backing up again we see that wise people "increase learning." These students have learned not just facts or academic information but the *knowledge* described in verse 7 ("The fear of the Lord is the beginning of knowledge"). Where did they learn it? From teachers who made this their singular goal.

Finally, notice where this begins: "A wise man will hear…" If your students would become helmsmen, you must get their attention. You must direct their minds from academia to theology. You must bring them face-to-startling-face with the majesty and glory of God in such a way that they are jolted from apathy and drawn to His multi-faceted beauty! That is your mission. Will you accept it?

Final thought: As a godly teacher, you should be developing students who will impact others for Christ.

Apple 8

PROVERBS 1:7

"The fear of the Lord is the beginning of knowledge: but fools despise wisdom and instruction."

Our Main Aim

Many scholars consider this verse the theme of Proverbs. It certainly is foundational to Christian education. Knowledge (here synonymous with wisdom as seen in the second half of the verse) begins with the fear of the Lord. Education begins when youth fear the Lord. Why, then, do we skip the beginning and concentrate on the results? We can educate all day, but we only educate fools unless they fear the Lord. As a teacher, my first objective is to bring my students face–to–face with God. How? 1) By relating everything that happens in the classroom to Him. 2) By linking every bit of information, every fact, every historical event, every formula, and every discipline taught to an attribute of God. 3) By drawing your students' attention to how God is at work in every problem your students face (whether related to home, school, or friends). 4) By drawing attention to the providence of God in everything that happens in the classroom. 5) By keeping a record of answered prayer in the lives of the students throughout the year.

Students' minds must be renewed daily by focusing their attention in the classroom on the presence and work of God. They must recognize His hand at work, love Him, and respect Him. This is where education begins. If this is not your first priority and the dominant factor in your classroom, you are educating fools. Ask God to help you turn your class into a "praise lab" of His glory.

Final thought: If students don't see the Lord in everything they study and in everything that happens in your class, you are giving them the wrong microscope.

Apple 9

PROVERBS 1:10

"My son, if sinners entice thee, consent thou not."

Youthful Naïvete

Solomon understood human nature. He knew that youth are naïve sinners. Solomon's warning reveals his understanding of two things:

1. Sin is enticing. All people are born with a natural bent to evil, our students included. This fascination puts them in a dangerous position.

2. Youth are naïve. Fascination with sin is exacerbated by the naïvete of youth. Solomon has already called them simple in verse four. He is not implying that they are dumb but that they do not have the experience to make wise judgements. Our students are not always rebellious. Sometimes they are just simple to the ways of the world.

This is a deadly combination. A four–year–old's fascination with a snake, coupled with his childish innocence, can prove deadly. So it is with our youth.

Solomon's understanding of these two forces prompts him to write a ten–proverb warning. The verses that follow reveal how temptation works and what must be done to overcome it. What forces "entice" youth to sin?

1. The need to belong ("Come with us" v. 11). The longing for belonging has led many into sin when their heart was not actually rebellious. Their naïvete caused their downfall.

2. The desire to possess. ("We shall find all precious substance" v. 13). All men want. The danger is being controlled by wants. It is not money that destroys a man but the love of it.

3. The failure to foresee. ("They lay wait for their own blood" v. 18). Youth do not see the end from the beginning. Their inexperience makes them shortsighted.

Final thought: Take time today to warn your students of these problems.

"If they say, Come with us, let us lay wait for blood, let us lurk privily for the innocent without cause: Let us swallow them up alive as the grave; and whole, as those that go down into the pit: Cast in thy lot among us; let us all have one purse."

The Need to Belong

Let's look more closely at those things that cause your students to give in to the enticements of sin. First, there is the need to belong. These three verses make this clear. Notice the five uses of *us* in this passage. Your students have a strong desire to be accepted. This is a part of nature and is not in itself rebellion. However, the forces of sin understand this drive and use it to seduce the naïve to fall in with the wrong crowd.

Look at your students. All of them want to feel accepted. Some are not accepted at home. Some are not accepted by their peers because of the way they dress, or because they are poor, or because they are not academically sharp, or because they are not athletic, or a thousand other reasons. These students feel ostracized and are susceptible to following anyone who will show them attention. This is obvious in verse 14 when the child is willing to give his cash to this wicked crowd in order to belong.

How does this apply to you? Be conscious of those students who seem to be on the outskirts. Unlovely as they may seem, even to you, make a point to draw them in and show them you love them and that they belong. Do not allow other students to make fun of them or to leave them out. Champion them before others. Use every small victory in their lives as a platform to complement them. It is better that they "throw in their lot" with you than with the ungodly who will only take advantage of them for their own gain.

Final thought: Make your classroom the "accepting place."

Apple 11

PROVERBS 1:13

"We shall find all precious substance, we shall fill our houses with spoil."

The Desire to Possess

The second force that makes students prime candidates to follow the wrong crowd is the desire to possess. All men want to possess. This longing for things is at the root of all kinds of evil (1 Tim. 6:10). It is not possessions that destroy, but the love of them. Paul reminds us, "But they that will be rich fall into temptation and a snare, and into many foolish and hurtful lusts, which drown men in destruction and perdition" (1 Tim. 6:9).

This force drives your students, and its power often overwhelms them. I have seen children driven to stealing because they wanted tennis shoes like all the other kids.

How can you use this principle in your class?

First, make sure you don't emphasize the importance of money, possessions, or career-mindedness in your classes. Few Christian students are pursuing vocational Christian ministry. Why? They are following the god of mammon.

Second, stress the value of sacrifice and submission. Hold up as examples those who gave up in order to serve God (e.g., Moses, Paul the Apostle, and William Borden).

Third, be an example of sacrifice yourself. Don't flaunt possessions. Don't honor those who do. Warn against the excesses of money. Teach them the corrupting influences of money. Use this verse to teach them the danger of pursuing wealth.

Finally, exalt Christian ministry above all treasures.

Final thought: Emphasize the fact that God is worth more than anything this world has to offer.

The Importance of Foresight

The sinners described in these verses had no foresight. They enticed naïve youth to follow them, yet they walked the path of their own destruction. Youth lack the ability to see beyond today. It is a sign of immaturity, not rebellion. Remember that your best youth can be enticed to the grossest sins because of their "innocence."

"Experience is the best teacher," we are told. Yet we could avoid much heartache if we would but listen to those who have had the experience. Solomon here warns the simple to look beyond the now. So we must do with our students.

Teachers, bare your hearts to your students. Be transparent. Share with your class those times when you didn't listen to experience and the sadness it brought you. Show your failures. Obviously, you don't have to dredge up sins best left dead. But you can demonstrate those times when you failed to see the end from the beginning and the consequences. Let them see that we all struggle but that this is no excuse for sin.

Teach them how to look at the end, not the beginning. Use Moses as an example (Heb. 11:23–27). Teach them of Lot. Would he have made those same choices had he seen the end of his life? He was driven by the lust of gain; he lived for the moment. He was driven by the desire for what looked best, yet it led to his destruction because he did not consider the future. Warn them that some may "lay wait for their own blood." Teach them Proverbs 1:24–32. Use examples (anonymously) from your own former students. Teach them to live "with eternity's values in view."

Final thought: The wise teacher shows her students the ends of their actions.

Apple 13

PROVERBS 2:1-5

"My son, if thou wilt receive my words, and hide my commandments with thee: So that thou incline thine ear unto wisdom and apply thine heart to understanding, Yea, if thou criest after knowledge, and liftest up thy voice for understanding; If thou seekest her as silver, and searchest for her as for hid treasures; Then shalt thou understand the fear of the Lord, and find the knowledge of God."

The Measure of Success

Verse 5 describes the goal of Christian education. We want to produce youth who understand the fear of the Lord and find the knowledge of God. Academic scores do not measure success in Christian education. The number of influential graduates we produce does not measure success in Christian education. Instead, the number of our graduates who fear the Lord and understand Him determines our success.

How do we produce God-fearing youth? Solomon presents several steps, which we will look at more closely over the next several days.

The First Step to Wisdom

First, youth must "receive my words." The search for wisdom begins by learning from someone else. You are the "someone else." The word *receive* means "to take, to grasp, to seize, or to take away." The teacher's job is more than simply getting students to pay attention, as hard as that may be. We have not taught until our students seize upon the truth and make it their own.

Don't work on attention techniques. Focus on reaching their hearts. Paying attention is only the gate that leads to what you're really after—a possessed heart. How do we do that? We get to their heart through our heart. Students seize their mentor's passion, burden, and fire. If you're burned out or cold in your heart for both the Lord and your subject, your students will have nothing to seize.

Final thought: Youth can't snatch fire from dead coals. How's your fire?

The Second Step to Wisdom

Students must hide the Word in their hearts. Once more we see the teacher's focus—the heart, not the head. Memorizing facts is only a tool, and the tool is not the product. We are not equipping youth with the tools they need in life; we are fashioning their hearts. We must readjust our thinking in education. Education is about wisdom, not knowledge. Knowledge is for the head and features memorization. Wisdom is for the heart and features internalization.

Hide translates the Hebrew "storing up" or "saving" (as when someone collects gold coins and places them in a security box for safekeeping). It is our responsibility to make Christ and His Word so thrilling and valuable that youth treasure the teaching of the Word and long for fellowship with Him. When our students treasure what we teach them about the ways of God, we are beginning to educate.

Today's youth, sadly, place little value on the things of the Lord. Why? There are many answers to this question: the celeberties in sports and movies who glorify the things of this world, parents who treasure things that vanish, and peers who are eaten up with materialism.

How do we fight these trends? We give them an example. We must treasure the Word. We must memorize it and meditate on it—and enjoy doing what it says! We must share our enthusiasm for the Word with our students. Share with them each day what you have memorized. Take out a golden verse and handle it in such a way that your students are in awe of your awe. Soon they will share what they have received in their daily devotions. Only then are you beginning to educate!

Final thought: Encourage and demonstrate the importance of hiding God's Word in your heart.

Apple 15

PROVERBS 2:2

"So that thou incline thine ear unto wisdom, and apply thine heart to understanding."

The Third Step to Wisdom

Two problems confront the modern teacher: 1) Truth is not always easy to understand; and 2) Students are increasingly less able to concentrate. Yet without understanding, youth have not learned. This verse teaches that a person must "incline" his heart to understanding. *Incline* translates the Hebrew word meaning "to stretch out, to spread out." Wisdom and spiritual understanding come by stretching out our minds to grasp truth.

Students who cannot concentrate cannot learn. We can blame the problem on TV, rock music, or modern culture; but blame doesn't solve the problem. We must teach the mysteries of God to an increasing number of learning disabled students.

Be very careful that you don't write off such youth as rebellious or problem kids. Often, the very youth who cannot concentrate in their subject matter can be led to have a heart for God. Peter was probably not the greatest student in Galilee High. He was probably "hyper–active" and always "mouthing off." Yet he had a heart that could be reached. Both Paul the scholar and Peter the scoundrel were greatly used of God. Why? Because God is concerned with the heart! Many who cannot stretch their minds to grasp subjective concepts have a heart that can be stretched out to wisdom. Your job is to find those hearts that will incline to the things of the Lord and fill them with the treasures of wisdom.

Final thought: Work on your students' hearts, and their heads will follow!

The Fourth Step to Wisdom

Prayer should be the centerpiece of your classroom. Too often we thrust prayer to the corner. We might begin our class with a quick perfunctory prayer, but there is no passion. We are better off not to pray in our classes than to pray flippantly or as though we're rushing to get it over with so we can get to the important part of our class—teaching the subjects at hand.

We do our greatest teaching when we pray. Prayer is the mirror to the soul. Our students see our passion for God (or lack thereof) when we pray. They hear our heart's cry when we pray. He who would be wise must know how to pray. Our students will learn how to pray when they hear us pray.

Charles Bridges, commenting on this passage, said: "Earthly wisdom is gained by study; heavenly wisdom by prayer." Remember that Christian education is about heavenly wisdom.

Do you pray aloud each day for your students in front of them? Do they hear you call their names? Silent prayer for them is not enough. They must hear that you care. They must see you bare your heart to God on their behalf. Students have had their lives turned around because they heard the earnest prayer of a teacher, a pastor, or a parent calling their name.

But don't pray fast or flippantly. It is not perfunctory prayer but passionate prayer that God hears and that impresses students. Cry for knowledge; lift up your voice to Him in a way that lets your students feel your passion.

Final thought: Today, in front of your students, ask God to give wisdom to (name the student). Ask God to give that student a hunger/passion/thirst for Him.

Apple 17

PROVERBS 2 : 4 – 5

"If thou seekest her as silver; and searchest for her as for hid treasures; Then shalt thou understand the fear of the Lord, and find the knowledge of God."

The Fifth Step to Wisdom

What do you treasure? Values are caught, not taught. If you value earthly things, those values will become your students' values. The teacher who influences a generation for God is one who internally values fellowship with the Lord above all the treasures of earth.

How do students see your values? Values are seen in what we talk about most enthusiastically. Values are seen in sacrifice. Values are seen by where we place most of our time.

- Students may think making A's is more important than loving God. Why? Because the teacher continually stresses grades but says little of the Lord in class.

- Students may think geography, history, or literature is more important than loving God. Why? Because the teacher is far more excited when teaching these subjects than when teaching the Bible.

- Students may think current events are more important than the Word. Why? Because the teacher never talks about her devotions or her prayer life but does share the morning news.

- Students may think sports are more important than loving God. Why? Because the coach emphasizes winning more than a godly spirit.

What do you treasure? How often do your students see you seeking the treasures of wisdom in prayer and the Word? Do students see you treasuring your relationship with Him? Only then will you "find the knowledge of God," and only then will your students "understand the fear of the Lord."

Final thought: Teachers must treasure the Lord.

Teachers Need Wisdom

Christian teachers know they need wisdom. Every day we are molding the lives and affecting the souls of precious children—the handiwork of God. We know we will stand before Him and give an account of how we affected their lives. Yet children differ in their backgrounds, home situations, and personal characteristics. How can we wisely deal with each one? The "wisest man who ever lived" (Solomon) tells us how to gain such wisdom. The answer? Go to the source of wisdom! "The Lord giveth wisdom: out of his mouth cometh knowledge and understanding."

Years earlier, Solomon was given the privilege of choosing a gift from God. Solomon chose wisdom, and his request was granted. Thus, Solomon passes his secret to us in this proverb. It was not Solomon who was wise but the God who gave him wisdom. If we would have the wisdom of Solomon we must go to the same source as Solomon.

Solomon asked for wisdom—perhaps this was the wisest thing he ever did. We need wisdom every day. Perhaps the wisest thing we will ever do is to ask God daily for the wisdom to deal with each child and each situation we will face that day.

Asking for wisdom is a humbling experience because it is an admission that we don't have all the answers and that the Lord alone is our sufficiency.

Final thought: Right now, humbly ask God for wisdom for this day, and make it a daily habit.

Apple 19

PROVERBS 2:10-11

"When wisdom entereth into thine heart, and knowledge is pleasant unto thy soul; Discretion shall preserve thee, understanding shall keep thee."

The Benefit of Wisdom

Yesterday's apple told us how to be wise. Today's apple tells us the benefit. What is the benefit of God's wisdom? Preservation. "Discretion shall preserve thee, understanding shall keep thee" (verse 11). *Preserve* and *keep* translate Hebrew words meaning "protect" and "guard." In Proverbs 2 the writer names two evils from which the wise are preserved and guarded: corrupt people (vv. 12–15) and immorality (vv. 16–21).

For our purposes, God's wisdom protects us from giving unbiblical advice, from exercising undisciplined discipline, and from displaying an uncontrolled temper to our students.

But notice the recipient of this benefit: "When wisdom entereth into thine heart…" The blessings of verse eleven are not for those who know the wise (right) thing to do, but for those who are governed by the wisdom they know. It is one thing to have wisdom, yet it is another for wisdom to have us. We can be wise in our head but unwise in our actions. We can know what to do yet fail to practice it in the heat of a classroom situation. Why? Because the wisdom we possess hasn't possessed us. Simply put, wisdom hasn't "entered into thine heart." Only those who are unconsciously controlled by God's wisdom experience its benefits.

And how does God's wisdom "enter into our hearts"? By spending much time in prayer and in meditation on the ways of God in the Word. Gradually, God's ways will become ours, and His wisdom will become the unconscious, controlling force in our classrooms. Then we will escape the tyranny of mechanically trying to do the right thing, or the tragedy of doing the wrong thing. God's wisdom will protect us from error. We will intuitively do the right thing!

Final thought: Make sure His wisdom has "entered into thine heart."

P R O V E R B S   3 : 3

"Let not mercy and truth forsake thee: bind them about thy neck; write them upon the table of thine heart."

Balanced Christian Character

Mercy (loving–kindness) and truth describe the full spectrum of Christian character. The balanced blending of these two qualities makes the most effective Christian servant. Mercy without truth leads to compromise, and truth without mercy produces harshness. Mercy must be fortified with truth, and truth must be tempered with mercy.

The second half of the verse parallels the first: mercy must be bound about the neck (as golden rings beautify the neck of a woman); truth must be written in our heart (learned, memorized, and practiced). Thus, the blend of mercy with truth makes us both attractive and intelligent in our dealings with our students.

God wants us to be attractive to our students. We must reveal the beauty of Christ in our dealings with our students. In Psalm 119 David speaks of blessed people who attracted him to the Lord (vv. 1–3). Harsh, cold, letter–of–the–law strictness does not attract students but rather grieves students (Matt. 23:4) and ultimately kills any desire they may have for the Lord (2 Cor. 3:6). We must ever be careful when we deal with student disobedience and failure to preserve our students' view of a loving, merciful God.

Truth, however, must not be sacrificed for the sake of peace. Sin must be confronted with God's Word. The wise teacher has so written the Word in his heart that he can skillfully and gently use it to construct his students' lives.

Final thought: The Word can be a hammer either to bludgeon or to build a life. If we use it without mercy, we may well destroy a child's desire for the things of God. If we use it with intelligence and mercy, we may build a life. "Lord, teach us how to mercifully use your Word to build lives for you!"

Apple 21

PROVERBS 3:5

"Trust in the Lord with all thine heart; and lean not unto thine own understanding."

Trusting God

It's so much easier to trust in ourselves than in God. The new teacher may trust in her training and education. The experienced teacher may trust in her experience and mastery of the subject. Others may trust their gifts or talents, but all this is forbidden. The Hebrew reads: "but toward your understanding do not lean."

Rather, we must place all our trust in the Lord. Charles Bridges calls this "the polar star of a child of God." This trust must be exclusive. No other confidence (in knowledge, skills, or experience) can exist in harmony with it. We are about a divine work, and we need divine help.

This trust must not only be exclusive; it must also be entire. It is a "childlike, unwavering confidence in our Father's well–proved wisdom, faithfulness, and love" (Bridges). Why should we trust in anything else? What is my knowledge compared to His? What is my understanding compared to the Creator's? What is my talent compared to His power?

The wise teacher must develop his understanding but never lean on it. To fail to develop our understanding in this age of technology and mass communication is sin, but to lean on that knowledge is a greater sin. The more we add to our knowledge and the more we develop our skills, the more God will use them as He sees fit. But the danger is that we will lean on them rather than trust God.

How do we know we are trusting God and not leaning on our education and experience? By the time we spend in prayer. Trust in God and distrust of self can be measured in direct proportion to the amount of time you find yourself asking God for help and guidance in fervent prayer.

Final thought: How much (or little) do you pray, and how much (or little) do you lean?

Knowing God

The Christian's greatest achievement is to know God. Paul declared "that I may know him" (Phil. 3:10) as the mark toward which he pressed.

Solomon puts it similarly: "In all thy ways acknowledge him." *Acknowledge* translates a Hebrew word first used in Genesis 3:5 where it is found twice: "For God doth *know* that in the day ye eat thereof, then your eyes shall be opened, and ye shall be as gods, *knowing* good and evil." Here are the two senses in which this word is used throughout the rest of the Bible: 1) to know in the sense of having information or facts, and 2) to know by experience. God knew the facts; Adam and Eve would know by experience. Thus, to acknowledge God is to know Him through His Word and through personal daily experience.

Know Him Through the Word

We grow in our knowledge of Him by spending much time with Him in prayer, and especially by meditating on Him in the Word. Your goal is not to study the Word of God but to study the God of the Word. Look for His character and His ways (how He operates) as you read the Word. Make two columns in a notebook. In one, record the characteristics of God you observe as you read, and in the other, record the way God operates in the passage you read.

Know Him Through Experience

Further, you must come to know Him experientially in "all thy ways." That is, every day, in every situation, and in every problem, you must consciously observe Him and mark what He did. Again, keep your thoughts in a notebook and review the notebook regularly.

Final thought: Faithfully seeking to know God will soon "direct your paths."

Apple 23

PROVERBS 3:6

"In all thy ways acknowledge Him, and he shall direct thy paths."

Don't Get Stressed

Knowing God brings blessings to the Christian. God promises here that He will direct the paths of those who acknowledge (know) Him. *Direct* literally means "make straight, level, smooth, or pleasant."

Wouldn't it be great if you could have a smooth and pleasant class? You can. At least it will seem smooth to you—even in the midst of problems. In fact, even the problems will become great opportunities for teaching your students the ways of God.

To acknowledge Him includes not only the idea of knowing how God works yourself but also communicating it to your class. See every situation as an opportunity to show your students how God is at work and how God worked. They may observe God waiting until the last moment to work in order to test our faith. They may observe God preparing the class ahead of time for something that they didn't know they would face. They may observe God answering prayer and healing a parent who faced a life–threatening situation.

It is your task to make certain you acknowledge Him before the class. Take advantage of every situation to throw the spotlight on God. Eventually, your class will begin looking for God's hand and expecting God to reveal Himself. Then your ways will be "smooth, level, straight, and pleasant." Even the problems will be exciting because you and your students will be waiting to see what God will do.

Final thought: To observe God in past experiences is to expect God to reveal Himself yet again in present experiences.

PROVERBS 3:9-10

"Honor the Lord with thy substance, and with the firstfruits of all thine increase: So shall thy barns be filled with plenty, and thy presses shall burst out with new wine."

Do You Give?

A Christian teacher doesn't have much substance and sees little increase, yet she is not excused from obeying this command. Some may think they are immune to sacrificial giving because they work for the Lord all week, but God's Word does not qualify this command. In fact, if we have a desire to glorify the Lord, we will count it a privilege to give Him the firstfruits of our increase.

The key is in the words *honor* (literally, glorify) and *firstfruits*. Giving comes from a desire to glorify the Lord and put Him first in our lives. The more we love Him, the more we want to glorify Him; the more we want to glorify Him, the more willing we are to give.

Firstfruits is a reminder of the principle that the first of everything belongs to God. The first day of the week is His. The eldest son was his. The first priority of our lives is His. In all things He is to have the pre-eminence. Israel gave the first portion of their income to the Lord. This became known as the firstfruits. It was a reminder to Israel that the produce they reaped was the gift of God and that the land itself was His. Thus, the higher I place Him in my priorities, the more willing I am to give him the firstfruits. This is why we count the tithe from our gross income rather than our net. If we tithe only on our net income, we give the government, retirement, and hospitalization the firstfruits.

We will never become poorer by giving. God promises that blessings will exceed our wildest expectations when we honor him with our gifts.

Final thought: If you would have a fruitful ministry, be faithful in giving Him the firstfruits of your income.

Apple 25

PROVERBS 3:12

"For whom the Lord loveth he correcteth; even as a father the son in whom he delighteth."

Delighting in Discipline

God corrects us because He loves us. A father corrects his son because he loves him. Teachers correct their students because they love them. We have already spoken about the need for a balance of mercy and truth in dealing with our students. This balance is seen in the word *correcteth*. There is a difference between correcting and punishing. Punishment repays a person for wrong behavior (truth without mercy). Correction seeks to remedy the behavior rather than exacting payment (truth balanced with mercy). Teachers do not punish; they correct.

Correction involves instruction and discipline, counsel and chastisement. (Proverbs 29:15 counsels, "The rod and reproof give wisdom…"). Too often we are long on the use of the rod but short on reproof. It is easier to give a demerit than it is to counsel. It takes little forethought to scold and less to punish, but neither shows love. Discipline without counsel reveals laziness and a lack of love.

- He that loves will counsel (unless he is too lazy).
- He that loves will bear his soul with a student (unless he is too lazy).
- He that loves will spend much time in scriptural guidance (unless he is too lazy).

Do we truly delight in our students, or do we endure them? He that delights in them will diligently avoid punishing students, and will conscientiously correct (instruct) them.

A word to principals is in order. No child should ever come to your office for discipline and leave without prayer and loving counsel. That counsel should continue in weeks to come. If you're too busy for this, you're too busy! Correction is your highest calling. Avoid punishment.

Final thought: Your ministry involves counseling.

Wise Counseling

Counseling comes in two flavors: wise and unwise. This verse identifies wise counseling (correction). How do we gain wisdom and understanding? We find it and get it. *Find* implies searching. *Get* translates a Hebrew word that implies receiving a gift.

But where do we find wisdom? Proverbs 8:35 tells us: "For whoso findeth ME…" Wisdom is in the Lord. "The fear of the Lord is the beginning of wisdom." In Christ are "hid all the treasures of wisdom and knowledge" (Col. 2:3). Thus, the pursuit of wisdom is the pursuit of the knowledge of Christ. And where do we pursue knowledge of Christ? Colossians 2:7 gives us a clue: "Rooted and built up in him, stablished in the faith…" Colossians 3:16 further explains it, "Let the word of Christ dwell in you richly in all wisdom…" Thus, we gain the wisdom of Christ by searching to know Him in the Word.

It is our privilege to counsel and correct youth by pointing them to God's Word, and especially to the nature, character, attributes, and person of the Lord, as revealed in His Word.

A teacher's most often used phrase in counsel should be, "What would Jesus do?" Or, "What does the Bible say?" Too often we give advice without any reference to Scripture. We say, "I think," but what we think isn't important. What God's Word says is all that is important. But to give that kind of counsel you must be wise in the Word and in the knowledge of Christ, and you must let it dwell in you richly. A wise counselor is one who knows how to analyze every situation in light of 1) who God is, and 2) what God says.

Final thought: Point your students to Scripture, not your thoughts, in every situation. Both you and the class will be blessed, for "Happy (blessed) is the man that findeth wisdom…."

Apple 27

PROVERBS 3:19

"The Lord by wisdom hath founded the earth; by understanding hath he established the heavens."

Science Tells Us About God

When we study the earth and space, we study God. Both are the product of God's wisdom and understanding. Christian education is unique in this perspective. It sees every discipline as a dramatic portrayal of the glory of God. Psalm 19:1 declares, "The heavens declare the glory of God, and the firmament showeth his handiwork." It is incumbent upon the Christian teacher to display God's glory in every subject—whether science, geography, history, math, or grammar. (Yes, even language reveals God's glory.)

God condemns the ancient world for not seeing God's glory in creation (Rom. 1). Do we make the same mistake? The wise teacher will look for God in everything. If we'll just take the time to look, we can see God's wisdom in plants, animals, dirt, trees, or anything else that He created. Consider math, for example. What character of God do we see reflected in math?

- God is organized. Math wouldn't make any sense if it wasn't.
- God is absolute. There are rules to math that cannot be broken (4+4 never equals 9, no matter what the postmodernists say).
- God is exclusive. Just as there is only one right answer in math, so there is only one God—there is no room for any other.

It is your responsibility to see God in everything you teach and to make sure your students see Him. How will you reveal God in each subject today?

Final thought: Instead of a daily lesson plan perhaps we need a daily God plan. "Today, I will reveal the following about God in history (math, geography, etc.)...."

Praise Your God

Think of the power in your hand! As a Christian school discipler you hold the mind, the heart, the soul, and the life of all the disciples in your class. Your speech or actions may help or hurt, encourage or discourage, or make or break each of those disciples. You have an awesome responsibility. How do we insure that we impact those disciples for the Lord?

This passage contains two thoughts. First, magnify the goodness of God. Second, honor those students who are worthy.

Would you agree that every child in your class is due the knowledge of the goodness of the Lord? Is there any greater good than His goodness, glory, and majesty? If we are to see transformed lives, our students must see the goodness of the Lord. Sadly, many disciplers know only how to present the severity of God. Children grow up thinking of God as a prison guard who will "get me if I get out of line." What goodness of God will you magnify today?

A second thought is also confirmed in this verse. Some of your students are due special honor. This is important because you get what you honor. If you honor righteous character, you will get it. Psalm 12:8 says, "The wicked walk on every side, when the vilest men are exalted." When we honor the wrong students (the cool, the ungodly, and the apathetic), we only multiply them. Sadly, many schools idolize the athlete and overlook the godly. Make sure you honor the faithful, the disciple who is struggling, but trying. Learn to encourage. Which students do you need to encourage? How will you "withhold not good" from them today?

Final thought: You get what you honor. Find ways today to magnify God's goodness and to honor the godly. It's in the power of your hand to do it.

Apple 29

PROVERBS 4:4

"He taught me also, and said unto me, Let thine heart retain my words: keep my commandments, and live."

Bible Curriculum

Verses 4–9 explain what Solomon was taught by his Father, David. "For I was my father's son…he taught me also, and said unto me." Today we enter David's home to hear how he taught his son. 1) He was anxious for his son (vv. 5–8). "Get wisdom, get understanding. Forsake her not, and she shall preserve thee. Wisdom is the principal thing, therefore get wisdom: and with all thy getting get understanding. Exalt her, and she shall promote thee." The repetitive nature of this passage exposes David's concern for Solomon's spiritual development. 2) He was more concerned for his son's heart than his head: "Let thine *heart* retain my words." (v. 4). He knew that words would be forgotten, but the heart would be remembered. 3) He made wisdom, not facts, the focus of his education (vv. 7–9). "Wisdom is the principal thing." Now we know why Solomon asked for wisdom when God offered to give him his desire.

What do we learn as teachers? We learn that we must be concerned for every child in our class. We are not just doing a job. We are impacting lives and investing in futures. We learn that our main task is the forming of a heart, not the informing of a head. Finally, we learn that true education creates a hunger for divine wisdom. That is the principal thing!

Final thought: Creating a thirst for God's wisdom is the teacher's principal task.

"Wisdom is the principal thing; therefore get wisdom: and with all thy getting get understanding."

Your First Priority

What is more important in your class: teaching facts or instilling wisdom? What do you test: memorization or understanding? According to this verse, wisdom is the principal thing. The Hebrew word for *principal* means "first" or "beginning." All true education begins with wisdom, not knowledge. Two thoughts emerge from this: 1) The teacher must be wise, not just knowledgeable; 2) The students must first be wise, then they can learn.

Before we can instill wisdom in our students, we must "get wisdom" (see also verse 5). If you do not know the Word and how to use it skillfully, you are not qualified to teach in a Christian school, though you may have deep knowledge of every other subject. Dr. A. C. Gabelein argues that all Christian teachers should have a double major including both their field of expertise and Bible. Why? Because we are teachers of wisdom, not merely facts. How much time do you spend in the Word each day? Do you plunge its depths and ascend its heights?

Understanding refers to the insight necessary to use wisdom skillfully. All problems should be approached with Scripture. Psalm 119:24 reminds us, "Thy testimonies also are my delight and my counselors." Notice the use of the plural "counselors." Every problem has a verse that addresses it. Your insight in using the Word will enable you to point your students to the Scriptures in every situation. Therefore, "get wisdom, and with all thy getting, get understanding."

How does this apply to our students? We must insure that they are wise before we insure that they know facts. How do we do that? We'll save that for the next apple.

Final thought: Are you wise in Scripture, and do you impart this wisdom to your students?

Apple 31

PROVERBS 4:7

"Wisdom is the principal thing; therefore get wisdom: and with all thy getting get understanding."

Applying Wisdom in Real Life

Today we apply yesterday's truth to the students in your class. Since wisdom is the first prerequisite in biblical education, we must insure that our students are wise before we insure that they know facts for a test or grade.

How do we impart the principal thing to our students? We must connect every situation to the Word of God. Ask yourself how you would relate the following classroom situations to Bible principles.

A student doesn't want to take his math test home to be signed by his dad. After talking to him, you find out that he is afraid his unsaved dad will spank him severely for his poor grade. Other students are aware of his refusal. What biblical principle(s) would you teach?

Two students in your class are best friends but recently have had a falling out. Now they cannot speak kindly to each other. What would you do?

One of your students is really down, so you inquire why. He tells you that last night his soccer coach in the city soccer league benched him the entire game because he missed some practices early in the season. It seems clear that the coach probably did overreact due to frustration. What do you teach that student?

One of your students starts crying in class. When you ask her why, she says that her grandma died over the weekend. She asks, "Why would God let my grandma die? We prayed for her, and she still died." What do you say to her and to the class?

In everyday situations you must guide the students to act with godly wisdom. You will teach more through circumstances than you will through curriculum.

Final thought: If your students leave you with knowledge and good grades but have not grown in biblical wisdom and understanding, you have failed.

"Exalt her, and she shall promote thee: she shall bring thee to honor, when thou dost embrace her."

Promoting Wisdom

Since wisdom is the principal thing for both student and teacher, we should "exalt her" and "embrace her." But how do we exalt wisdom in the classroom?

1. Talk about wisdom and explain what it is. The first weeks of the school year should stress the difference between knowledge and wisdom. Explain that wisdom is the right use of knowledge. If you train an unwise student, you might be training a future enemy of mankind. Students should be wise before they learn.

2. Show the results of wisdom. Proverbs is full of promises and blessings to those who are wise. Stalin, Hitler, and Bin Laden were all brilliant, educated men, but none had godly wisdom. They perverted their knowledge and used it to bring great devastation to the world and to themselves.

3. Take advantage of opportunities to teach students to practice wisdom. Sometimes the best thing you can do is to forget your curriculum for a moment. Then, biblically and wisely deal with a situation, and lead the students to see why this is the right thing to do. Don't force it on them; help them discover it for themselves.

4. Urge your students to embrace it (see today's verse).

How to Embrace Wisdom

1. Study it—spend time each day discussing what the Bible says about it.

2. Meditate on it—develop a wisdom notebook for each student, and assign a verse for them to reflect upon and write about each day.

3. Pray for it—James said we should ask for wisdom. Pause for prayer daily.

4. Practice it—you should have a mental barrel full of situations that you turned into wisdom–making moments.

Final thought: Exalt and embrace wisdom!

Apple 33

PROVERBS 4:23

"Keep thy heart with all diligence; for out of it are the issues of life."

Guard Your Heart

The most important item in the classroom is the teacher's heart. Two Hebrew words in this verse describe our responsibility. The first is translated *keep;* the second is translated *with all diligence.* Actually, the first word means *of all guarding;* the second means simply *guard.* Thus, the Hebrew says, "Of all the things you guard, guard your heart!" The picture is that of a watchman on a wall looking diligently for the enemy.

How careful are you about your heart? Of all your concerns, your heart matters most. Why? The heart is the well–spring from which all our motives, actions, words, and attitudes flow. Therefore, your classroom will reflect your heart.

How to Guard Your Heart

1. We should daily fill our heart with the water of the Word. Psalm 1:1–3 describes the prosperous (happy) man as one who is "planted by the rivers of water." In verse 2 David defines the planting: "But his delight is in the law of the Lord and in his law doth he meditate day and night." As we plant ourselves by the rivers of God's Word, we begin the process of keeping our heart.

2. We should evaluate our heart daily to see if any enemy has entered. Satan infiltrates our heart through our eyes and ears. If we protect what we see and guard what we hear, we will keep our heart.

3. We should exercise godly thoughts. Meditate on a verse from Scripture each day. Meditate on an attribute of God for five minutes. What is the attribute, how did Christ show it, and what does it mean to my life? Can I manifest that attribute in some measure today? Conclude with prayer, thanking God specifically for the things you have learned. Finally, write down your thoughts in a journal and review them often as a reminder.

Final thought: Guard your heart if you would teach your students the way of life.

Watch Your Words

Some students have been turned off to Christianity because of the insensitive words of a teacher. First Thessalonians 5:14 teaches us that there are three kinds of problem youth: the rebellious, the weak, and the easily discouraged. Of these, only the rebellious are hard hearted. They have made up their minds that they don't want any part of Christianity.

Many more are easily discouraged. Although they are not rebellious, they act as though they are. How are they different? When you get them alone, they will say things like, "I want to be right with God. I've tried to do the right thing, but it just doesn't work for me." This is the sign of the easily discouraged person who wants to do right but doesn't have the character and fortitude to follow through. Failure devastates him.

What do you do for him? He needs encouragement, not discouragement. For him words of affirmation and confirmation are far more powerful than words of condemnation. Condemning words will devastate the person with a sensitive, easily discouraged personality.

Finally, the weak student, like the easily discouraged, is differentiated from the rebellious by the desire to live for God. He has tried it, but he doesn't seem to have the strength. The Hebrew for *weak* indicates one who is "small souled." He just doesn't have the strength to stand against the world. How is he to be treated? The Scriptures say, "Support the weak." Give him a person to lean on. He needs strong companions who will run with him and help pull him away from the ungodly crowd.

Final thought: Your tongue will either discourage and devastate the easily discouraged and weak or snatch them from drifting into the crowd of the rebel.

Apple 35

PROVERBS 4:26

"Ponder the path of thy feet, and let all thy ways be established."

Taking Inventory

This verse has close ties to verse 23, "Keep thy heart with all diligence." Not only must we take inventory of our heart, we must also take inventory of our steps. The paths of our feet are not just the physical places we go but also the direction in life we are going.

First, where do you go in a day? The places you go may be undermining all the wisdom you are developing in school, home, and the church. The friends with whom you walk may be teaching you ways that are not established. Each of our students should be concerned about with whom they walk and where they walk.

Second, in which direction are you headed? Are you growing in the Lord? Can you say you are closer to Him today than you were six months ago? Can you say you have a deeper passion for the Lord than when school began? Are you making progress, or are you slipping backwards? Ponder the path of your feet. If you keep going as you are now, where will you be in ten years?

The last phrase challenges us to "let all thy ways be established." That is, make sure your ways—the things you do and say—are establishing character, building a stronger heart for God, and turning you into a stalwart champion for Christ. Are you establishing your ways?

Final thought: Are your ways establishing your life to better know God?

PROVERBS 4:27

"Turn not to the right hand nor to the left: remove thy foot from evil."

Are You Living What You Teach?

Consistency is important in a teacher. The right way is a narrow way. If I turn left or right, I endanger my walk. My shoes will be muddy. Grime and dirt will splatter on my pants. All whom I teach will see it. My inconsistency will undermine my own teaching. Students will see the dirt on my feet and realize I have no authority to tell them to walk a straight path.

The teacher's life is closely watched by students. Are you faithful in church? Are you faithful in devotions? Do you find yourself happily talking about the Lord to your students? Do you find that you work the Lord into every situation in class?

On the other hand, Proverbs says, "remove thy foot from evil." Do you lose your temper and discourage the easily discouraged or fail to support the weak? Do you practice what you preach?

We can't tell our students to be faithful in church when we aren't. We can't tell them to flee worldliness when we persist in listening to music that is so close to the world that people can hardly tell the difference, or when we watch movies that are filled with words and ideas we would not allow in our classroom.

Final thought: We must practice what we teach. Consistency is needed in order to have an impact.

Apple 37

PROVERBS 5:21

"For the ways of a man are before the eyes of the Lord, and he pondereth all his goings."

God's Evaluation

Ways translates a word that means "directions." *Goings* translates the Hebrew for "wagon tracks" (worn ruts, indicating repeated travel). *Pondereth* means "to weigh, to examine."

In summary, both a person's direction in life and the things he does repeatedly are seen, evaluated, and examined by the Lord. Nothing in our life goes unnoticed by Him. We stand before the eyes of the Lord.

Does it strike you that God sees and weighs everything you do? He knows the direction you are taking—whether you're drifting off course, whether you're slipping backwards, or whether you're growing closer to Him.

The writer of Proverbs uses this verse at the conclusion of a warning concerning immorality. He reminds young men that God sees all, knows all, and carefully evaluates and weighs their souls.

This should cause you to face your school day carefully. God will be in that class. He will weigh all you say and how you treat the easily discouraged, the weak, and the rebellious. He will evaluate how much you practice Scripture in situations that arise. He will observe the passion with which you teach your students about Him. He will observe how much you sacrifice yourself to lift them up and encourage the easily discouraged with Scripture and positive cheerfulness. He will be concerned with how you support the weak with scriptural help and personal involvement.

Final thought: Yes, someone more important than the principal will be in your room today and every day. What will He see? What will He write on His evaluation slip?

PROVERBS 6:1–2

"My son, if thou be surety for thy friend, if thou hast stricken thy hand with a stranger, Thou art snared with the words of thy mouth, thou art taken with the words of thy mouth."

The Power of Words

Words are critical. They can heal or wound; they can edify or destroy. Wrong words are especially destructive in the classroom because young, impressionable minds are at stake. Although this passage addresses unwise promises, the principle applies to many situations. We can also be snared in the classroom with authoritarian and sarcastic speech.

One of a teacher's greatest temptations is an authoritarian spirit (and tongue). Because teachers are supposed to know all the answers, they can easily develop an "I'm right, you're wrong" attitude, which is contrary to a Spirit–filled heart. Even when students are clearly at fault, the Bible tells us to rebuke them "in love" and "in a spirit of meekness" (Gal. 6:1), "considering thyself…." We must remember that we also are sinners. James reminds us to "be swift to hear, s–l–o–w to speak, slow to wrath." Are we not often guilty of blurting out words that we later regret? "Slow to speak" may be the fastest way to problem solving, while "hasty speech" most often is the slowest way to develop a life.

Sarcasm is another snare. Ephesians 4:15 admonishes us to speak the truth in love. Yet we often speak the truth—in sarcasm; or we speak the truth—in pride. Such words as *stupid, dumb,* and *idiot* should not be part of a teacher's vocabulary. Such unloving words are darts that pierce the hearts of youth.

Finally, we must be careful what we promise—whether it is a blessing or a bane. As Jephthah made a rash promise (Judges 11:30–31), so teachers must guard against a flash of temper in which they accuse, judge, or sentence a student before they have gotten all the facts and had time to cool down.

Final thought: Be s–l–o–w to speak in every classroom situation. Run every word through a scriptural filter.

Apple 39

PROVERBS 7:1–2

"My son, keep my words, and lay up my commandments with thee. Keep my commandments, and live; and my law as the apple of thine eye."

How Important Is God's Word to You?

Apples are a teacher's gift. Early in American education, students (coming from an agrarian culture) had little else to give a teacher. Thus, the apple became a symbol of education. However, the *apple* mentioned in Proverbs 7:2, is not the apple of educational lore.

The word here translated *apple* is the Hebrew for "pupil" of the eye. The passage teaches that we are to keep and protect God's Word with the same intensity and sensitivity that we protect our eyes. Think about it—does anything cause a quicker hand and eye reaction than when an object flies at our eye? Our eyes are the most sensitive part of our bodies, and our natural instinct is to protect them at all costs.

Christian teachers are here instructed to keep God's Word with the same sensitivity they have for their eyes. The best "apple" for a classroom is the Word of God. But do we keep it? Do we lay up God's commandments in our classroom?

When a situation arises, do we use the written Word as the authority, or do we use our words? When students struggle with a subject, do we use Philippians 4:13 to make them a believer? When students fear a test, do we quote verses that give them courage, or do we shame them for being afraid? When students misbehave, do we show them which verses of Scripture (or biblical principle) they are violating, or do we simply rebuke them? When God answers prayer, do we show them that God's Word works?

Final thought: Perhaps the greatest thing we can teach our students is that God's Word really does work! It is meant to be practiced, and when it is practiced, it will bring blessings to our lives. But to teach this truth, we must emphasize it. Used effectively and constantly, God's Word will keep your classroom healthy and wise.

PROVERBS 8:6

"Hear; for I will speak of excellent things; and the opening of my lips shall be right things."

Excellent Speech

Are you worth listening to? Think of it, your students have to listen to you all day every day. Solomon here encourages his students to listen ("hear") because he speaks of excellent and right things. Only excellent and right words are worth listening to.

What is excellent speech? The word *excellent* in this passage is found 48 other times in the Old Testament, and in every other instance it refers to leaders or nobles. Thus, excellent speech is that which is noble and worthy of our submission. It is something worth listening to.

In a classroom, excellent speech is that which is salted with the Word of God. The teacher worth listening to applies Scripture to the classroom throughout the day and shows the student that God's Word really is at work in their class.

Excellent speech comes from a teacher who is so thoroughly saturated with the Word that he can hardly speak without quoting it. Excellent speech is not forced but is natural to a teacher who spends time every day reading the Word, memorizing it, and meditating on ways to apply what he reads to the classroom.

Excellent speech seizes upon every opportunity to ask the class, "What does the Bible say about (so and so)?" The "so and so" can be a wrong reaction from a student, an expression of fear, a prayer request, an argument, a derogatory action by one student toward another, or a classroom subject. Dozens of opportunities to bring God's Word to bear upon classroom events occur every day. If we speak apart from the Word, as good as our words may seem, our speech is not excellent and right and is thus not worth listening to.

Final thought: Only God's Word is excellent and right. Make sure you and your classes are full of it!

Apple 41

PROVERBS 8:11

"For wisdom is better than rubies; and all the things that may be desired are not to be compared to it."

Developing Values

Christian teachers are in the business of values clarification. The world, peer groups, and some parents are guilty of instilling wrong values in children. It is the teacher's job to restructure the students' value system and change their frame of reference. (Romans 12 calls this "renewing the mind.")

Today's society is materialistic. Its most valuable things will not last—cars, houses, bank accounts, fame, and power ("all the things that may be desired"). Students see materialism on TV and in movies; they see it practiced at home; they hear it from their peers. Thus, they come to your class with little regard for spiritual wealth.

Yet God's Word declares that "wisdom is better than rubies." Two thoughts come to mind: 1) Do your students believe this? 2) How can you change their value system?

How can you renew the values of your students? First, you must be sure your life in front of the students is an example of in which God's truth is valued over man's riches. What do you talk about around them? Is your life one of material pursuit, or pursuit after God?

Second, you must purposefully show your class why practicing God's Word is worth more than gold. Do you encourage them to pursue vocational Christian service? Do you apply Scripture to every situation? Do you give illustrations of those that violated God's truth and paid the consequences? Do you give examples of the blessings of following God's Word?

Final thought: Your students must leave your class with a deeper love for God's Word than when they entered. If they do not, you have failed.

Thinking like Jesus

Most Bible scholars interpret "wisdom" in Chapter 8 as the personification of Jesus Christ. If that's the case, then Christ is saying, "Counsel is mine, and sound wisdom: I am understanding; I have strength." If this interpretation is right, then both teacher and students must come to know Jesus in a deeper way than just salvation. That is only the first step in obtaining true wisdom. Matthew 11:29 urges, "Take my yoke upon you, and *learn of me*…." Paul's ambition was "That I may know him…" (Phil. 3:10).

How deeply do you know the Lord? Do you spend time meditating on His character, His attributes, and His ways? If you do, you will have counsel and sound wisdom, and your teaching will be transformed. Your advice will be the excellent speech we discussed a few days ago.

If you understand how Christ thinks, you will have deeper understanding in every situation. If you get to know Him, you will have strength to face every problem, discouragement, and trial in your life. Further, you will find that your teaching will have greater power and force as you constantly imitate His ways and quote His words. Remember, He said, "I have strength."

Final thought: "What Would Jesus Do" is more than a bracelet to wear. It is a principle that must govern our class. But to practice it, we must know Him deeply and intimately.

Apple 43

PROVERBS 8:30

"Then I was by him, as one brought up with him: and I was daily his delight, rejoicing always before him."

Jesus' Delight

Proverbs 8 is a picture of Jesus personified as wisdom. This verse is especially noteworthy. Christ here claims that during the creation of the world He was "by" and "brought up with" the Father. The words are reminiscent of John 1:1: "In the beginning was the Word and the Word was with God, and the Word was God." The phrase *brought up with Him* comes from the Hebrew meaning "a craftsman." That is, He was involved in the creation process with the Father. Further, Christ claims that during the creation of the world (verses 27–29), He was present and delighted daily in what His Father was doing, rejoicing always in His presence.

Do we have such delight in the Lord? The phrase *daily His delight* is literally "daily delight." If Jesus delighted daily in the Father, should not we? What is your daily delight? We should make it our business to find one attribute or act of God in which we delight daily. Are there not enough divine attributes and actions to last us a lifetime?

In verse 31 Christ is seen "rejoicing in the habitable part of his earth" and in "the sons of men." Here then is how we should teach science and nature—by displaying and rejoicing in the creative glory of God. Do we talk about the stars, or do we talk of the glory of God in the stars? Do we speak of the history of man, or do we show the sovereignty of God in history? Do we teach English, or do we show the marvelous God who created all languages and divided the world into language groups? If we do not teach the glory of God in science and nature, we do not accurately teach science and nature.

Final thought: What is your daily delight? Do you love teaching because you get to show the glory of God in each subject you teach? Make Him your daily delight.

PROVERBS 8:34

"Blessed is the man that heareth me, watching daily at my gates, waiting at the posts of my doors."

What Are You Waiting For?

Wisdom (Christ) continues to speak and promises to bless those who watch "daily at my gates, waiting at the posts of my doors." It is one thing to determine to delight daily in the Lord, but it is another to know how. How do we watch and wait daily at His gates and doors?

First, we must watch. The first step in meditation is to learn to open our eyes and ears to what God is saying. This includes full attention to what we read, but it also requires asking God to teach us. Psalm 119:18 begs, "Open thou mine eyes that I may behold wondrous things out of thy law." This should be our daily prayer as we open the Word.

Second, we must watch and wait. We must be willing to spend time studying one passage until we understand what it says and what it means. Waiting requires patience. Watching requires working over each word and phrase with diligence. Meditation demands time and toil. A cursory reading of the Word will miss the true beauty that is there. If I am to be blessed, I must be willing to take the time and make the effort to pore over the Word.

Third, we must watch and wait daily. Delighting in the Lord is not a one–time requirement. It is a daily privilege, and only those who daily practice it will learn true Wisdom. Consistency in the Word brings blessing.

Finally, we must watch and wait daily at His gates and doors. One waits at a gate to see the owner come and go. Thus, the focus of our meditating is not on the Word of God, but on the God of the Word! How do we do this? Each day, choose a verse or passage of Scripture and record in a notebook what you see and learn about the Lord. Don't focus on other things—just focus on Him.

Final thought: Do you want a blessed class? Practice waiting daily at His gates.

Apple 45

PROVERBS 9:10

"The fear of the Lord is the beginning of wisdom: and the knowledge of the holy is understanding."

True Education

In commenting on the parallel verse in Proverbs 1:7 we stated, "we can educate all day, but we only educate fools unless they fear the Lord!"

Here, however, Solomon adds, "and the knowledge of the holy is understanding." *The holy* is understood by most scholars to refer to God. Thus, the fear of the Lord is coupled with knowing God. True education begins with knowing God. Herein is the key to understanding philosophy, math, physics, the sciences, sociology, and history.

A teacher's great task is to know God and to make Him known. Only as your students gain a deeper appreciation of the "Holy One" will they correctly understand the disciplines of the classroom.

Our text emphasizes the holiness of God in this connection. God is not just a creator; He is a holy creator. All that He has created is holy, and only when seen in that light will mankind understand life. Students must learn that they cannot succeed if they live their lives apart from the Lord. They are holy (separated) unto Him. He made them, He owns them, and He requires their submission. It is precisely this point that evolutionists resist. Thus, they have invented an alternative origin to the universe. A leading scientist once said, "To admit that there is a God carries with it certain psychological and sociological implications that we are not ready to accept." What are those implications? If there is a creator God, then we are all under His authority. Colossians 1:16 speaks to this: "all things were created by him and for him." It is that last phrase that brings true understanding. The road to wisdom begins with the acknowledgement that we exist *for* the delights of a holy creator God.

Final thought: It is your job to bring your students to an acknowledgement of the need for total submission to God as the Lord of their lives.

"He that gathereth in summer is a wise son: but he that sleepeth in harvest is a son that causeth shame.

Wisdom in Harvesting

There is a time to reap and a time to sow. This truth is as evident in the classroom as on the playground. There are times when students are ready to learn, and there are times when they are not. You waste your time and theirs when you do not realize this. Don't aimlessly drone on while the students' minds are elsewhere. Likewise, there are times when the harvest is ripe, but we are so tied to our lesson plans that we miss it. When students start asking questions (even when it isn't about what you're teaching), they are probably ripe for harvesting. A harvest moment has occurred in your class and you mustn't be asleep. Be prepared to "run a rabbit trail," drop what you're teaching, and see where the discussion leads. Jesus was an "occasional" teacher. When people asked him questions, or when he passed a field, tree, vine, or other scene, He seized the moment and used it to teach a lesson. Yes, this kind of teaching is unstructured—but it is most effective. It is taking advantage of the "summer" of the students' minds and harvesting true understanding.

Are you awake to those moments when the class is ready for a harvest? It may be a child ready for salvation. It may be an off–the–wall question. It may be a recent national, local, or personal event. Each of these present summer moments, and you must be alert to harvest.

Final thought: The teacher who is stuck to a lesson plan has no time to harvest. Summer comes in fleeting, unplanned moments in students' lives. Stay awake, stay flexible, and harvest.

Apple 47

PROVERBS 10:11

"The mouth of a righteous man is a well of life: but violence covereth the mouth of the wicked."

Wisdom in Speech

If we could only think this way every time we get discouraged or want to quit. The mouth of the Christian teacher should be a well of life to her students. Since we are indwelt by the Holy Spirit, who is "a well of water springing up into everlasting life" (John 4:14; 7:38), our speech, when controlled by Him, is holy and powerful.

Not so are the teachers who don't know the Lord. They teach at worst vain philosophies that ultimately will damn the soul, and at best they teach a wisdom that is only temporal and earthly.

But Christian teachers have a special privilege. Their words can transform lives, save souls from destruction and hell, rescue youth who live in dysfunctional families, and encourage those who have given up.

It is not our duty simply to impart knowledge. Rather, it is our privilege to give life. We are life-savers.

How do we speak with such power? We do so by filling our own heart with the refreshing waters of the Spirit. Not every Christian teacher speaks with such power. It is only that teacher who each morning fills her heart with the Word of God and surrenders her body each day to be filled with the Spirit. Only by prayer and the indwelling of the Word do we become a life-spring of refreshing water to our students.

Final thought: Do your words transform lives? Is your well full or empty?

Dealing with Sin

Students will fail. Like the teacher, they are sinners. How we deal with their sin is vital to their future. Although chastisement for sin is taught in God's Word, this verse focuses on other aspects of dealing with sin.

First, we must not aggravate sin. A principal's or teacher's attitude, words, or spirit toward a student may provoke them to sin more. Paul reminds fathers to "provoke not your children to wrath" (Eph. 6:4). Teachers can so lose it in dealing with students' failures that they provoke the student to greater sin. When we lose our temper, yell at students, or jerk them around, we convey a spirit of hatred which "stirreth up (aggravates) strifes." Rather than help the student, we drive them further from the Lord. This is a sure sign of hating our students.

Other reactions that stir up sin include gossip, criticism, or acting as though we are shocked that a Christian could do such a thing. Paul admonishes us to restore those who sin with a spirit of meekness (Gal. 6:1).

If we truly love our students, we will cover their sin. To cover sin does not mean that we ignore it, or that we hide it from others so as to avoid chastisement. Rather, the Hebrew word means "to cover with something else." When we help students overcome their sins, we cover them. *Cover* in this context refers to restoration. We cover sin when we take God's Word and show them how to conquer it—whether it is dishonesty, a critical spirit, a gossiping tongue, laziness, procrastination, or a thousand other sins.

Final thought: Do you hate or love your students? The answer is seen in how you respond to their sin—and how they respond to you!

Apple 49

PROVERBS 10:14

"Wise men lay up knowledge: but the mouth of the foolish is near destruction."

Wisdom in Devotions

Wise men store up knowledge for future use. We have seen this truth before in Proverbs 2:1, 7; and 7:1, which admonish the wise man to hide or lay up God's Word. Here again the wisest man who ever lived advises us to store up knowledge.

What does this mean in practical terms? It means more than to have devotions or to memorize verses. A storehouse is most useful when it is organized, so God's Word is most useful when each verse is stored for a particular purpose. The teacher faces many situations in the course of a year: students who are discouraged, fearful, immature, rebellious, hungry for God, inattentive, hyper–active, given to mischief, learning disabled, and struggling with temptation. Likewise, the teacher faces her own problems, frustrations, discouragements, and temptations.

How do we handle them? We show wisdom when we store up specific verses for specific needs. As you read the Word each day, keep three notebooks handy: an Arsenal, a Treasury, and a Courthouse. Each time you read a verse that deals with a particular sin, write the reference and verse in the Arsenal, and note in the margin the sin it attacks. Each time you find a promise, write it in the Treasury, and note the situation where this promise would help. Each time you find a principle that would help in making right choices, record it in the Courthouse with an explanation of its use. Memorize the verses; meditate on them frequently.

Final thought: Rich teachers both store and organize God's Word to use it effectively with their students. Does your counseling come from God's storehouse or from your mind?

PROVERBS 10:19

"In the multitude of words there wanteth not sin: but he that refraineth his lips is wise."

Wisdom in Holding Our Tongue

There are numerous references to the tongue in this chapter with each one approaching it from a slightly different perspective. Proverbs 10:19 considers the value of holding our tongue (or the sin of speaking too much).

The more we speak, the greater the chance of sin. We are sinners, and we show it most quickly in our speech. Thus, the wise teacher will learn to refrain his lips. We sometimes do this when we are around other teachers in the lunchroom or on the playground. What is the topic of our conversation? Do we pour out our frustration over certain students or things we don't like in the school? Do we talk about the parents' failures or how impossible some students are?

Over the course of a year these conversations become a "multitude of words" as each teacher is encouraged by the others. We must be advised that "in the multitude of words there wanteth not sin." The innocent sharing of frustrations soon leads to discontent. The students are aware that the teachers are talking about them, and this leads to further disunity. Low morale among both students and teachers is soon to follow.

The wise teacher will not engage in such conversations, nor will he or she be part of such groups, for "he that refraineth his lips is wise."

Final thought: What do you talk about when you are with other teachers, at lunch, or on the playground? Does it encourage a passion for God, or does it encourage discontent?

Apple 51

PROVERBS 10:29

"The way of the Lord is strength to the upright: but destruction shall be to the workers of iniquity."

Wisdom in Meditation

What is the Christian teacher's strength? Proverbs 10:29 answers: "The way of the Lord." If the way of the Lord is our strength, then we need to ask, "What is the way of the Lord?"

The way of the Lord is how God operates or thinks in a given set of circumstances. Those who are married learn the way their spouse acts or reacts in certain situations. So the way of the Lord is how the God of the universe acts in various situations.

How do we learn the way of the Lord? We learn how God thinks and acts by observing Him. As we read the Word, we need to look for the ways God acts. Here is the secret to life–transforming meditation. As we read the Word, we focus on God in the story. What is the situation? How did God respond? How did God think? As we do so, we discover what makes God happy, what displeases Him, and what He will do in a given circumstance. Discovering these truths will give us wisdom to respond in similar situations. Observing God's ways will increase our faith as we see His care, provision, and power in the trials of life. Noting the way God operates will help us make wise decisions.

Do you want to keep another journal? Besides your Arsenal, Treasury, and Courthouse, you need a Ways of God journal. This may be the most important one of all. What better exercise for a teacher than to spend time lovingly observing the infinite, matchless ways of God?

Final thought: Don't study the Word; study the God of the Word. No exercise is wiser. No exercise will make you stronger.

"The righteousness of the perfect shall direct his way: but the wicked shall fall by his own wickedness."

Wisdom in Character

Christian educators sometimes emphasize good minds rather than good hearts. However, character is an infinitely better possession than talent or genius, but it is of corresponding rarity. Yet, it is character ("the righteousness of the perfect") that shall direct our way.

What exactly is this thing called character? Bishop Butler, two centuries ago, wrote that character is "…those principles from which a man acts, when they become fixed and habitual in him." Our character is composed of those thoughts and actions that have become a permanent part of who we are.

Fortified with this information, look back at our apple. "The righteousness of the perfect shall direct his way…."That is, character will direct or determine the way we act. Thus, we see a circle. We begin with meditation on the immaculate character of Christ. This is the heart of "putting on the new man."Then, we seek through grace to imitate His character in our life. When these acts of meditation and imitation are consistently practiced, they become habits, which in turn become character. In this way, we develop the mind of Christ, and thus, His righteousness will direct our ways. This is the wisdom of character.

Final thought: What directs your way? Are you controlled by your own selfish flesh, by the expectations of others, or by the inward character of Christ in your life?

Apple 53

PROVERBS 11:5

"The righteousness of the perfect shall direct his way: but the wicked shall fall by his own wickedness."

Wisdom in Character Development

The same verse that applies to the teacher also applies to the student. Our students are developing patterns and habits in their lives that will shape character and will guide them the rest of their lives. These habits and patterns may be righteous or unrighteous. Laziness and sloppiness both begin with bad actions that become habits. Irresponsibility and inattentiveness start with actions that lead to habits that finally become character.

What can a teacher do? It is not enough to get after the students or to punish them. We must break the chain of action. First, we must show them the righteousness (character) of Christ. What is Jesus like? How would He act? These are questions we must constantly put before our students.

Initially, we must lead them to repeatedly take right actions in order to develop right habits in their lives. They must first learn to do right because it's what Christ would do. At they mature, they will begin to do right because of their relationship with God.

Is this easy? No. It's hard. But it is accomplished with small steps. "For precept must be upon precept, precept upon precept; line upon line, line upon line; here a little, and there a little" (Isa. 28:10). Teachers, begin with a list of Christ's qualities and work on them with the class: kindness, gentleness, consistency, obedience, serving others, meditation, prayer, and putting others first.

Final thought: The first habit you need to develop in your students is the habit of prayer and meditation. You should plan a time every day when your students practice these exercises. Practiced often enough, devotions will become a habit. Later, this will be part of their character.

"By the blessing of the upright the city is exalted: but it is overthrown by the mouth of the wicked."

Wisdom in Words

Nothing is as powerful as the tongue. Here it is compared to great armies. An army may spend months besieging a city, only to have the siege fail. Yet a single word from a wicked man may bring that same city to its knees. Likewise, blessing the just and honorable citizens of a city will do more for its establishment than great battlements and walls. Thus, the tongue may be used to build up or to tear down. We must insure that our tongue is used for the former.

Here we see the power of praise. A word of encouragement may be the turning point in a child's life. Simple compliments like, "You have a talent for writing," or "You are a very thoughtful person," may do more for that child than all the scolding or admonishing in a lifetime.

How do we turn our classroom into an "exalted city?" We do so by blessing the students and by teaching them how to bless their fellow students. Your classroom must become a city of praise where all the citizens love and care for each other.

The teacher of such a classroom must guard against destructive speech. Criticism, making fun of another student, gossip, and derogatory remarks about other classmates should be immediately stopped, and the students should be reminded of this or similar verses. "What does the Bible say?" should be the first words from your mouth when you hear destructive speech. Soon, the act of praising will become a habit, and the habits will become character.

Final thought: Turn your class into a city of praise by modeling it before your students and by teaching them how to praise.

Apple 55

PROVERBS 11:12

"He that is void of wisdom despiseth his neighbor: but a man of understanding holdeth his peace."

Knowing Your Students

Why does a person despise his neighbor? He lacks wisdom or understanding of his neighbor. Lack of knowledge about another often leads to unwise and unjust criticism.

A wise teacher knows her students. She doesn't just know their names, she also knows them. She knows their home life, she knows their strengths and weaknesses, she knows their likes and dislikes, and she knows their capabilities and those areas in which they struggle. This knowledge causes her to refrain from criticism or unrealistic expectations.

The unwise teacher may know these facts, but she doesn't take them into account when dealing with the student. Though she may only despise the ways of the student, the student may think the teacher despises him. Thus, "he that is void of wisdom despiseth his neighbor…" (at least in the eyes of the neighbor.).

Do you know the background of your students—their home situations (are his parents unsaved, is she being raised by her grandparents, are his parents divorced, does her father have a drinking problem)? Do you know their hot buttons—that which will encourage them to give 100%? Do you relate to their interests (sports, cars, art, music, etc.) and encourage them, and do you use these as illustrations in teaching? Do you seek to understand why they are always late, why they don't do their homework, or why their mind wanders in class? Perhaps a family fight the night before kept them up until midnight.

Final thought: It's easy to despise problem students, but the wise teacher will take the time to get to know and understand why they behave as they do.

"A talebearer revealeth secrets: but he that is of a faithful spirit concealeth the matter."

Wisdom in Honoring Confidentiality

A teacher has privileged information. She knows her students' grades, their IQs, and their scores on tests. Parents and students alike may confide in her, telling personal secrets. In each case two things are involved: trust and vulnerability. Those who confide both trust the teacher and make themselves vulnerable to the teacher's trustworthiness. If the teacher is faithful, the confidentiality will be honored. If the teacher is not faithful, trust will be broken.

The promise of confidentiality can present moral dilemmas. What if the information given is of a nature that others must be told due to the seriousness of the problem or other circumstances? Must the teacher then honor the promise of confidentiality?

First, the teacher should never give a carte blanche promise of confidentiality. It is wise to tell students before they confide in you that if you deem it necessary you will have to tell their parents or other authorities. Second, if you have already promised confidentiality and then find that you must tell others, you should first notify the one to whom you promised confidentiality and tell them why you must break the promise. Even then, only those who must know should be told. In most cases, however, you will have no reason to tell others. In those cases a faithful teacher will tell no one, not even her best friend, with whom she shares everything.

Final thought: When we betray someone's confidentiality, we destroy their trust, and we show them that we don't value them. In so doing, we violate Scripture and dishonor the teaching profession. Be a faithful teacher, not a talebearer.

Apple 57

PROVERBS 11:14

"Where no counsel is, the people fall: but in the multitude of counselors there is safety."

Wisdom in Counsel

Teachers (and principals) don't know everything. As wise as they are, they still need help. Proverbs reminds us on several occasions to seek counsel before we act (15:22; 20:18; 24:6). Although too much advice can hinder the planning process, more advice is usually better than less. Here is another reminder that humility is part of true wisdom. Those who don't seek advice think they are wise, while the truly wise seek advice from "as wide a circle as practical" (Complete Biblical Library). If we don't seek advice, we are warned that those we lead will fall. But where should we go for counsel?

First, a Christian teacher should seek counsel from the Lord. David cries "I will bless the Lord, who hath given me counsel" (Ps. 16:7). This implies prayer and seeking God's face. Prayer is yet another sign of true humility. The more I realize my own insufficiency, the more I pray. The more self–sufficient I feel, the less I pray. God, through the Holy Spirit, stands ready to give us divine insight if we will ask.

Second, we must turn to the Word. Psalm 119:24 declares, "Thy testimonies are also my delight and my counselors." You will note that *counselors* is plural. God's Word is filled with counselors. Every verse is a counselor for a particular problem. Here again we see the need to fill our Arsenal, Treasury, Courthouse, and Ways of God notebooks with godly counsel.

Finally, we should seek counsel from godly peers. Don't imitate King Ahaziah who sought the counsel of the advisors of Ahab (Israel's most wicked king), "to his destruction" (2 Chron. 22:4).

Final thought: The wise in heart are humble in heart. They seek the face of the Lord through prayer, meditation, and time in the Word before they set upon any action.

PROVERBS 11:17

"The merciful man doeth good to his own soul: but he that is cruel troubleth his own flesh."

Wisdom in Showing Mercy

Mercy is the flip side of grace. In grace I get what I don't deserve. In mercy I don't get what I do deserve. Biblical mercy is a divine enablement. It is the fruit of the Spirit. This mercy is not showing pity in words or in looks, rather it is showing kindness and love from the depths of our heart when a student or offending person is in trouble. Mercy does not avoid chastening, but when the chastening is done, mercy continues to show kindness and love toward the one chastened. Mercy is not just an attitude but an action of loving-kindness toward the offender. God chastens believers for their sin, but in His mercy He continues to love and care for us, offers full forgiveness, and continues to shower us with blessings.

Christian teachers must not hold grudges or withhold deeds of kindness to those who oppose them. Parents may misjudge us, or students may criticize our actions. In each case we must continue to show love, care, and kindness toward those who don't understand. Such displays of mercy are beyond our natural ability. It is only as we are filled with the Spirit that we can exercise true loving-kindness toward those who give us a hard time.

Finally, Proverbs teaches us that those who are merciful do good to their own souls. Charles Bridges reminds us, "The merciful man will always find a merciful God" (Ps. 41:1).

Final thought: "In watering others with our mercy, our own souls 'will be like a watered garden'" (Charles Bridges, Proverbs).

Apple 59

PROVERBS 11:22

"As a jewel of gold in a swine's snout, so is a fair woman which is without discretion."

Wisdom in a Pig's Snout

Character is everything! Youth do not know this. Their emphasis is on the outward appearance—clothes, hair styles, possessions, looks, athletic ability. Yet these are but vain things that fade with the years.

It is our job to impart this wisdom to our students. But how? First, we should give them biblical examples. Saul was outwardly impressive, but he lacked character and ended his life in disgrace. He was a gold jewel in a pig's snout. Paul was nearly blind, was not an orator, but had great character, and God used him mightily.

- Lot had possessions but no character.
- Abraham had possessions and character.
- Moses turned his back on wealth but had great character.
- Daniel was a captive, but his character advanced him to second in the kingdom.

Next, we must take advantage of situations that arise in our class to teach proper values to our students. Each month, have your students work on a different part of the fruit of the Spirit. Define it, have them find verses of Scripture about it, and as situations arise ask: "Is that the way we show love (or whichever part of the fruit you are exploring)? What could 'John' have done instead of what he did? How should 'John' have responded? Why?"

Encourage the students to report when they see one of their classmates demonstrating that trait. Honor those who demonstrate character over appearance during the month.

Final thought: Your goal is not to bejewel pig snouts, but to change snouts into something beautiful!

Wisdom in Discernment

There is a time to teach, and a time to refrain from teaching. Charles Bridges says, "Every truth is not therefore fitting for every person or for every time." God revealed His Word gradually. While Christ was on earth, He on occasion charged his disciples "that they should tell no man that he was Jesus the Christ" (Matt. 16:20). Later he told them, "I have many things to say unto you, but ye cannot bear them now" (John 16:12). Christ often spoke in parables to the public but explained the meaning when he was alone with the disciples. David declared that he spoke to those "that fear God" (Ps. 66:16).

This truth must be remembered in dealing with youth. There are truths that are meaningless to a child until he is saved. Most cults have been started by ungodly men who had been taught Christian doctrine. What does this mean for a teacher? First, we must make certain our students know the Lord. Then, we must carefully explain the truth as students are capable of hearing and accepting it. To force truth on those who refuse to accept it is to feed pearls to swine. It will inevitably produce a rebellious student, hardened against the things of God.

Preaching standards and forcing outward holiness on the unregenerate and rebellious youth will only embitter them toward God. Students must be led, not driven, to accept truth and holiness. At the first signs of rejection, they should be taken no further. When they come to accept that truth, they may be further informed. Thus, they are taught line upon line, precept upon precept as they accept the lines and precepts.

Final thought: Teachers must be discerning and sensitive to the spiritual limits of their students. They must never seek to take them beyond their spiritual receptivity.

Apple 61

PROVERBS 12:25

"Heaviness in the heart of man maketh it stoop: but a good word maketh it glad."

Wisdom in Encouragement

It is the Christian's privilege to encourage rather than discourage. Joseph encouraged his brothers by speaking kindly to them in spite of their treatment of him (Gen. 50:21). Moses encouraged Israel by the Red Sea (Exo. 14:13). The Lord encouraged Israel (while warning of their imminent captivity) with these wonderful words: "For I the Lord God will hold thy right hand, saying unto thee, Fear not; I will help thee" (Isa. 41:13).

Christ Himself set an example of encouragement. We find encouragement on His lips as he healed the man sick of the palsy (Matt. 9:2), as He walked on the water before his frightened disciples (Matt. 14:27), and when he told the disciples that even the hairs on their heads were numbered (Matt. 10:30).

The Holy Spirit is called the *paraklete,* meaning "to encourage, to comfort, to console." Thus, when we are filled with the Spirit, we will encourage our students. In 1 Thessalonians 5:14, Paul admonishes us to "warn them that are unruly (rebellious), comfort (encourage) the feebleminded (easily discouraged), support the weak, be patient toward all."

Find ways to encourage your students. Praise them for small victories; teach them the promises of God (Phil. 4:13; Isa. 41:13; 1 Thess. 5:24); comfort them when they fail. Challenge them with examples of underdogs who won (Moses—speech impediment, David—lowly shepherd, Amos—fruit–picker, Peter—uneducated fisherman, and Matthew—hated tax–collector).

Final thought: Good words make a glad class ("a good word maketh it glad")! Are your students encouraged or discouraged when they leave your class? Remember: Satan discourages, while God encourages.

PROVERBS 13:4

"The soul of the sluggard desireth, and hath nothing: but the soul of the diligent shall be made fat."

Wisdom in Dreams and Diligence

It's good to be a dreamer. It's better to be a doer. Nothing is accomplished without a dream, but dreams don't make it happen. Many desire to grow spiritually; they want to have power with God. But such power cannot be purchased—it must be earned. There is no other way to learn the Word apart from study. There is no other way to acquire knowledge apart from concentrated effort. Here is a principle students must learn. It is not the dreaming but the doing that matters.

We live in an age of shortcuts. We have instant potatoes, instant coffee, instant tea, and instant gratification. We can go to the internet and find whatever we need—instantly. Thus, we want quick solutions to grades and godliness. Adam thought that by simply eating a piece of fruit he would be godly. What a concept—instant godliness! But it didn't work. There are no shortcuts to godliness, character, or success. God told Joshua that good success would come if he would meditate in the Word day and night (Josh. 1:8). That implies work, consistency, sweat, and perseverance. Today's youth must be taught the value of sweat–equity. Character and godliness do not come by chance, or by dreaming, but by diligent effort.

Final thought: Little or nothing of value is acquired instantly.

Apple 63

PROVERBS 13:7

"There is that maketh himself rich, yet hath nothing: there is that maketh himself poor, yet hath great riches."

Wisdom in Priorities

Why do you teach? Obviously, if you're teaching in a Christian school, it is not for wealth! There are a thousand places you could teach and make more money. There are those who work for wealth yet are miserable. They have the houses, cars, and possessions that we think are nice, but in gaining these they have lost their families and true happiness. Fathers, pursuing their fortune, have lost their sons and daughters. Parents, seeking to increase their wealth, have found themselves spiritually bankrupt, divorced, or broken in health. They made themselves rich, yet they have nothing.

However, Christian teachers and others who invest their lives in youth make themselves poor yet have great riches. They count as their wealth young men and women who are now serving the Lord as preachers, teachers, Christian business-men, and leaders in their churches. It is far better to impact a life and drive an older car than to destroy a home and drive the latest sedan. Take courage, teacher. Invest in the lives of your students and you will have "great riches." You will have eternal, rather than temporal results.

Final thought: True wealth is measured in lives saved, not in dollars saved.

Wisdom in Disagreements

If you're alive, you will have disagreements. You will not always agree with the administration, another teacher, parents, or students. How we handle those disagreements will prove our character. When driven by pride, disagreements engender strife or contention. When driven by wisdom, disagreements lead to counsel. Bridges notes, "The desire of preeminence (3 John 9); revolt from authority (Num. 12:2); or party spirit (1 Cor. 3:3–4)—all produce the same results." Thomas Scott wrote: "Some point of honor must be maintained; some insult must be resented; some rival must be crushed...; some renowned character emulated; or some superior equaled and surpassed." These all stem from pride and cause disunity in our ministry.

The proud man believes he is wise enough. He asks no counsel and thereby proves his lack of wisdom. But the wise man knows that he knows not enough. He will seek the counsel of wiser men. He will allow himself to be misjudged or misunderstood rather than stir up strife. Philippians 2:3 admonishes us, "Let nothing be done through strife or vainglory; but in lowliness of mind let each esteem other better than themselves."

When you disagree, seek counsel from God, from His Word, from wiser men, and from the one with whom you do not agree. Often the disagreement is over misunderstanding or misinformation.

Final thought: It's natural to disagree. It's sin to contend!

Apple 65

PROVERBS 13:16

"Every prudent man dealeth with knowledge: but a fool layeth open his folly."

Wisdom in Responding to Disobedience

Those who think before they act are wise. Those who don't think reveal their foolishness. This axiom may be applied to how teachers respond to student misbehavior or disobedience.

Do you tend to reprimand students immediately, or do you get the facts before you act? We may see something we think is wrong and immediately respond by rebuking or admonishing the student, only to find that things were not as they seemed. We have revealed ("layeth open") our folly!

Better that we approach all apparent misbehavior or disobedience by first asking questions. "John, what did you say?" "Susan, what did you do?" "Why did you do that?" "What did you mean?" "Is this what I am hearing you say" (then repeat what you think they meant)?

Let's say school has a rule that shirts are to be tucked in at all times. A student is working in the concession stand during a ballgame and unloading crates of drinks. While working, his shirt gets pulled out. A wise teacher sees him and gently reminds him of the rule. A foolish teacher jumps on his case and then goes to the principal or writes him up for demerits. What was foolish about the second teacher's reaction? The circumstances were not considered. A teen, trying to help his school, temporarily forgot about the rule. The foolish teacher treated it as though it were rebellion. She acted without knowledge.

Final thought: Get the facts before you react! Display wisdom, not folly.

"He that walketh with wise men shall be wise: but a companion of fools shall be destroyed."

Wisdom in Companions

The obvious application of this verse is to walk with wise men. But let's think more of this. Who is wiser than God? Since God is all–wise, we would be wise to walk with Him!

In Genesis 18:17–19, God reveals His friendship with Abraham. He is determined to let Abraham know that He plans to judge Sodom and Gomorrah. Thus God asks, "Shall I hide from Abraham that thing which I do?" Why is there such intimacy with Abraham? Abraham walked with God. Matthew Henry suggests: "He was a friend and a favorite," and "The secret of the Lord is with those that fear him" (Ps. 25:14; Prov. 3:32). Henry adds: "Those who by faith live a life of communion with God cannot but know more of his mind than other people" (Hosea 14:9; Ps. 107:43).

Further, Abraham is given special insight because "He will command his children and his household after him" (v. 19). God gives special wisdom to those who both walk with Him and are committed to teach the next generation the secrets of the Lord! As teachers we have two thrilling privileges: 1) to become an intimate companion of God, and 2) to teach our students what He teaches us.

Final thought: We must learn to be a friend of God. We must walk with Him in intimate prayer and meditation. Then, we must learn to share our passion for our Friend with our students.

Apple 67

PROVERBS 13:24

"He that spareth his rod hateth his son: but he that loveth him chasteneth him betimes."

Wisdom in Discipline

Balance is necessary in discipline. On the one hand we must be understanding, we must take time to get all the facts, and we must not make rushed or rash decisions. Yet we must discipline misbehavior. Showing mercy does not exclude discipline. If we truly love students, we will discipline them; however, we must be certain that our discipline is disciplined.

Undisciplined discipline is as wrong as lack of discipline. If we are to discipline in a godly manner, we must do the following:

- Get all the facts before we discipline
- Counsel the student using Scripture passages that will help him overcome his problem
- Assure the student of our love and concern for him
- Pray with him and ask God to give us wisdom in giving the proper discipline
- Administer the discipline in a prudent fashion

He that "loveth him chasteneth him betimes." *Betimes* translates the Hebrew for early—before the disobedience becomes a habit. Parents mistakenly let their children get by with inappropriate actions until they become habits; then, too late, they try to discipline.

Final thought: Wise teachers see improper actions developing and deal with them before they become habits through careful scriptural counseling and other appropriate action.

"Where no oxen are, the crib is clean: but much increase is by the strength of the ox."

Wisdom in Growth

Growth costs. Every step forward requires a sacrifice. Solomon, writing to an agrarian culture, reminds Israel that when a farmer doesn't own oxen, he has a clean barn but no food. If he wants to eat, he will have to endure the toil of constantly cleaning a messy barn. So take your pick—plenty to eat and a dirty barn, or a clean barn and starvation!

Charles Bridges comments, "God works by *means,* not by *miracles.* We must take good care of the farm, if we want an abundant harvest…Spiritual fields, too, where there are no laborers, remain empty."

So it is with a Christian teacher. We can make more money somewhere else. We can avoid all the hassles of parents, apathetic youth, and grading papers late at night. We can have more time to take care of our house. But we will not see changed lives. If we want to impact the souls of tomorrow's leaders, we must be willing to have a dirty barn.

Sometimes that barn is our house. We have little time for cleaning and cooking. We may not have the best furniture. Our Saturdays are reduced to giving the house a once-over. But that may be the trade-off for godly youth.

Final thought: Dirty barns are sometimes necessary for clean hearts!

Apple 69

PROVERBS 14:10

"The heart knoweth his own bitterness; and a stranger doth not intermeddle with his joy."

Wisdom in Judging Others

Every man is an island. The deepest emotions (bitterness and joy) can't be fully understood or expressed by the soul. Everyone knows himself as no one else does. No two of us are alike; and these differences of mind, character, and emotions prevent perfect understanding, even in the closest friendships.

Eli totally misjudged Hannah, and instead of comforting, he rebuked one who needed understanding (1 Sam. 1:10–14). Gehazi harshly rejected the Shunamite woman and started to push her away from the man of God through his ignorance of her bitter sorrow. Fortunately, Elisha had better insight and declared, "Let her alone; for her soul is vexed within her" (2 Kings 4:27). Job's friends misunderstood his heart and proved to be worthless physicians and sorry comforters (Job 13:4; 16:2).

Teachers must be careful when they rebuke their students. They must not assume that the outward action is a true manifestation of evil or good within. Only God's Word and the Holy Spirit can adequately pierce to a person's inner needs and struggles, for only the Lord knows what is in man.

We must bring students to one point: "What does the Bible say?" Taking students to the Bible and applying specific verses to every problem or situation allows God to apply the Word to their deepest thoughts and motives.

Final thought: We don't know what our students are really thinking and feeling, but God does. Let the Word rather than your opinion be their help.

"Even in laughter the heart is sorrowful; and the end of that mirth is heaviness."

Wisdom in Discernment

Things are not always as they seem. A student's laughter may hide deep feelings of sorrow, abuse, or anger. A self–assured bravado may cover feelings of insecurity and worthlessness. A lack of concentration in class may reveal unresolved conflicts at home or elsewhere. A wise teacher will get to the heart of the issue and will show the student how to overcome it biblically.

When an honor student in science could not pass his reading comprehension test, a wise teacher asked, "What was your mind doing when you were reading the story?" The student's reply revealed resentment toward a male teacher who had expelled him from a class for something he didn't do. The deep unresolved conflict manifested itself in a lack of concentration. After reading several verses on forgiveness, the wise teacher asked him what the Bible said he should do. The student, understanding what the verses taught, responded, "Oh, no. I could never do that." Later, however, he went to the teacher and resolved the conflict. His problem was deeper than a lack of concentration. His problem was disobedience to the Word. His feelings of guilt interfered with his concentration.

Final thought: Your mission is to get beyond symptomatic problems. You must discover the root problem and lead students to deal with it biblically.

Apple 71

PROVERBS 14:17

"He that is soon angry dealeth foolishly: and a man of wicked devices is hated."

Wisdom in Reactions

Derek Kidner writes, "To see a situation calmly is to see it clearly." Here we see the sin of irascibility—acting on the state of our feelings, not the merits of the case. It is sin to be governed by feelings. A Christian's standard is to be "filled with (controlled by) the Holy Spirit." When anything else controls us, whether it be our emotions, our peers, the flesh, or substances (alcohol, drugs), we violate Scripture. God alone must control our actions and reactions. A loose tongue and a quick temper are signs of foolishness in the heart because they are proof that God is not in control. When we scream at students, make rash judgments, or display quick anger, we reveal that self, rather than God, controls us.

Further, quick tempers often lead to "wicked devices." Bridges puts it this way: "But sin grows from weakness to willfulness." A man who at first is "soon angry" may later become cruel and calculating in planned malice.

If you have a problem with making quick judgments, with a short temper, with overreacting, or with yelling at your students, you have a problem with "my rights and my way." Surrender your mind, your emotions, and your temper to God. Fill your mind with Scripture that deals with the sin of quick judgment and the wisdom of temperance. Memorize and meditate on the following verses: Proverbs 14:17, 29; 16:32; 19:11; Psalms 37:8; Ecclesiastes 7:9; and James 1:19.

Final thought: "Be not hasty in thy spirit to be angry: for anger resteth in the bosom of fools" (Eccles. 7:9).

Wisdom in Confidence

What a great verse for both parents and teachers! Those who fear the Lord become hiding places or places of refuge for their children. Many blessings are associated with fearing the Lord. The one highlighted by this verse is "strong confidence," or in the Hebrew: "the strength of security." Fathers who fear the Lord conduct themselves in a way that causes their children to feel safe and secure. The stability of the parents makes the home their place of refuge. The children love their home. They would rather be there than anywhere else!

The same is true of a teacher who fears the Lord. She manifests a security of strength that attracts students for advice and counsel, for prayer, and for assurance. Her class is a refuge for her children. Students sense a wisdom that will protect them from "deadly snares" (v. 27 and 13:14).

What does it mean to fear the Lord? It is to know Him so well and to be so saturated with His Word that your words, your actions, and your spirit reflect Him in everything you do.

Final thought: Your relationship with the Lord should be so strong and evident that your students feel safe and secure in your counsel.

Apple 73

PROVERBS 15:1
"A soft answer turneth away wrath: but grievous words stir up anger."

Wisdom in the Face of Anger

This verse, like many in Proverbs, seems too obvious to mention. The Proverbs, however, are given to increase insight. What insight do we gain from this verse?

First, it is never becoming for a Christian to be angry. In fact, a Christian should be adept at deflecting anger ("turneth away wrath").

Second, anger is most often stirred or quieted with a single tool—words! Words can both turn away anger and stir up anger.

Third, we must listen carefully to those who are angry so that we can respond with soft words rather than grievous words. We should always ask ourselves, "Do I really understand why this person is upset? What words will stir up his anger, and what words will soften his anger?"

Fourth, we must be in control of our own emotions so that we can be calm in the face of wrath. Proverbs 25:28 reminds us, "He that hath no rule over his own spirit is like a city that is broken down, and without walls." Such a city, in Solomon's day, was defenseless. When we lose control of our temper, we open ourselves up to trouble.

Final thought: "Let your speech be always with grace, seasoned with salt, that ye may know how ye ought to answer every man" (Col. 4:6).

"The tongue of the wise useth knowledge aright, but the mouth of fools poureth out foolishness."

Wisdom in Using Knowledge

Knowing is not enough. We must know how to *use* what we know. An unwise teacher may misuse knowledge to the detriment of the students, while a wise teacher will use knowledge "aright."

How can knowledge be misused? Some use their knowledge to twist Scripture and give it an unintended meaning.

Knowledge may puff up (1 Cor. 8:1), causing a teacher to display an air of superiority over her students. Statements such as "because I said so" or "do you think you know more than I do?" are a dead giveaway of a proud teacher. Such teachers may browbeat students or show contempt for their actions or answers. Thus, "the mouth of fools poureth out foolishness."

A more common problem is to use knowledge in place of Scripture. This can be a major problem with Christian teachers. Though we know the Bible, we don't always apply it to our students' lives. How do you handle a student who suffers from fear, anxieties, pride, anger, bitterness, lack of concentration, a broken home, social deficiencies, and so on? Do we know how to use the Scriptures or do we suggest they seek counsel? Does not God's Word tell us, "Thy testimonies also are my delight and my counselors"? If the Word of God is sufficient, then why do we use human reasoning to help our students? The purpose of teaching is not to dispense facts but to touch lives! We must meet children's problems head–on with scriptural principles, or we have not used knowledge "aright."

Final thought: Knowledge is a powerful tool. It can build or destroy. Ask God for wisdom to use it correctly.

Apple 75

PROVERBS 15:2

"The tongue of the wise useth knowledge aright, but the mouth of fools poureth out foolishness."

Wisdom in Using Knowledge Aright

Our last devotional dealt with the wrong use of knowledge. Today we consider how to use knowledge "aright." How do we use knowledge aright?

Right use of knowledge will creatively apply scriptural truth to students' lives. The Bible is not a fact book—it is a life book. Students may learn facts, but if they are not taught how to live those facts in real life situations, they do not have proper knowledge. When I face fear, what do I do? When my parents divorce, how do I handle it? When other students do not accept me, how do I respond? How do I handle guilt for things in my past? How do I handle abusive talk leveled at me? How do I grow in the Lord? These are questions that must be answered with the Bible. Right teaching will show your students what the Bible says about these and a thousand other internal problems our students face.

Right use of knowledge will exalt God in all we teach. Our students must see the majesty of God in science, nature, history, geography, government, and the arts, as well as in Scripture. Jesus accused the Pharisees of searching Scripture but not seeing the Lord in it (John 5:39). Students must be dazzled with the majesty of God rather than be in awe of our knowledge.

Final thought: To use knowledge aright we must analyze our students' needs, study the Word for answers, and make the Bible central and practical.

"A wholesome tongue is a tree of life: but perverseness therein is a breach in the spirit."

Wisdom in Mending Broken Walls

James reminds us that the tongue can destroy or give life. Here we are told that the tongue that gives life is wholesome. The Hebrew word translated *wholesome* means "to heal" or "to restore" that which is broken or hurt. Conversely, the perverse tongue breaks the spirit of another.

Teachers must be healers and restorers. Many of our students come to us with breached spirits. The language of Proverbs pictures a castle wall that has been breached in siege warfare allowing the enemy to rush in and capture the defenseless citizens.

A healing or restorative teacher looks beyond the untoward actions and words of their students and sees breached spirits that need mending.

More importantly, the restorative teacher seeks to mend (heal) those broken walls with wholesome words. The following are among the "healing words" (wholesome words) a restorative teacher will use: God knows and cares, God is able, God is here, God made you, and God placed you in your family. A restorative teacher takes time to counsel from the Bible, and shows students how to apply Bible truth to rebuild their "walls." A restorative teacher asks questions rather than provides lectures. "What did you do? What made you say that? What should you have done? What do you think the Bible says about this?" These are but a few of the questions you should ask as you help the student rebuild the walls of his spirit.

Final thought: Learn to be a wholesome (restorative) teacher!

Apple 77

PROVERBS 15:17

"Better is a dinner of herbs where love is, than a stalled ox and hatred therewith."

Wisdom in Love

Two thoughts race side by side in this verse: 1) Money is not always the most important consideration; and 2) Things are not always as they seem.

In Solomon's day, ownership of an ox indicated wealth and success. Yet Solomon reminds us that there are things far more important than wealth.

Today's youth are pressured to accept a materialistic value system. Christian teachers and parents may unwittingly add to this pressure by showing partiality to those who are better looking, who display athletic, academic, or artistic skills, or who exhibit polite and cooperative behavior. Yet appearance, ability, and even behavior may have little to do with the condition of a child's heart. Solomon warns that those who use flattery and smooth words may, in fact, have something to hide.

This brings us to our second thought: things are not always as they seem. Lot chose on the basis of appearance and ruined his life. That which looked great from a distance was a mirage. Two hundred yards from the Jordan the land was too saline to support vegetation. What appeared rich was, in fact, poor.

A child's life is just the same. Smiles may hide sadness. Laughter may cover tears. A nice home may harbor strife. Good behavior may hide a devious heart.

Final thought: Teach your children the truth of Luke 12:15. Life does not consist of possessions. Don't equate godliness with politeness. The good citizen of the school may not be a good citizen in heaven!

"The heart of the righteous studieth to answer: but the mouth of the wicked poureth out evil things."

Wisdom in Thoughtful Counsel

A quick response is often a sign of pride. When we think we know it all, we speak on impulse. When we realize we are but sinners, we don't trust our tongue.

Righteous teachers do not "pour out" their thoughts. They do not snap at their students. Rather, "the righteous studieth (ponders) to answer." But what must we ponder and how? First, we must search the Scriptures asking, "What does the Bible say about this situation?" Everything we say, and the way we say it, must be in agreement with Scripture. Second, we must study the person involved (student, parent, co-worker). We must consider what they said or did and what they really meant. We must consider other situations they may face that affect their actions or reactions. Finally, a righteous teacher should pray and seek God's face before answering.

Lou Priolo, commenting on this verse, writes: "It is often necessary to invest extra time, effort, and thought in selecting just the right words to express which biblical injunctions have been violated, which additional passages may be cited to support the indictment, the questions that will be asked of the child, and the manner in which the reproof will be administered."

Final thought: Think twice before you speak once. Your words can destroy more quickly than they build up!

Apple 79

PROVERBS 15:30
"The light of the eyes rejoiceth the heart: and a good report maketh the bones fat."

Wisdom in Our Face

We not only have to look at our students all day, but they also have to look at us. Solomon states that what our students see in our faces and hear with their ears is important. This verse, if paraphrased for teachers, might read: "A bright face and good news make for a healthy class."

The Bible speaks of two aspects of the face: its affective nature and its reflective nature.

As to its affective nature, Solomon says, "A merry heart doeth good like a medicine…" (Prov. 17:22). Your face will affect the atmosphere of your class! If you want a changed class, change your face! How? By considering the reflective nature of the face.

The face is a mirror of the soul. "A merry heart maketh a cheerful countenance" (Prov. 15:13). Cain's sin caused his countenance to fall. Moses' countenance shone brightly after his encounter with the Lord.

But what is the source of a happy countenance? Is it not the Lord, shining in our heart? David proclaimed, "They looked at him (the Lord) and were lightened (Hebrew—to sparkle, be cheerful)" (Ps. 34:5).

The Bible describes God as the Sun of Righteousness "arising with healing in his wings." If we would have a shining face, we must have the *Son* shining in our heart!

Final thought: A Son–filled heart makes for a happy face, and a happy face makes for a healthy class! Fill your heart with Him, and both your countenance and your words will be like sunshine in your class!

Wisdom in Our Face

Our last devotional spoke of the affective and reflective nature of our face. We discovered that our face both affects our class and reflects what is in our heart.

Sometimes we lose our smile and become frowning teachers. Problems in our private lives, difficult students, sickness, and a tired body all tend to wipe the joy from our faces. Yet these may be excuses for a deeper problem in our hearts.

A frowning face is often the result of sin within. Occasionally my wife asks, "Why are you frowning?" Usually it is because I'm either worried (the sin of faithlessness), frustrated (the sin of a wrong focus), I have too much to do and not enough time to do it (the sin of over-commitment), or I simply frown out of habit (I've frowned so many months that even though I have nothing about which to frown, I still do). Whatever the case, I am not reflecting a heart that is filled with the joy of the Lord, and it affects my family. What must I do? I must deal with my sin.

First, I must search my heart and the Word to find the reason for my joyless face. Then, I must confess and forsake my sin and ask God to "restore unto me the joy of my salvation." Finally, I must get my focus back on my all–sufficient God and glorious Savior and bless Him for His many benefits (Ps. 103).

Final thought: As the Jewish leaders took note that the disciples "had been with Jesus," so will your class rejoice when your face reflects the glory of the Lord!

Apple 81

PROVERBS 15:31
"The ear that heareth the reproof of life abideth among the wise."

Wisdom in Helping Students Listen

Wise students listen, but wise teachers produce good listeners. It is incumbent on Christian teachers to insure that their students "hear the reproof of life." But how do we get youth—with a thousand things to distract them—to listen?

First, we must care that they listen. A godly teacher has a passion for two things: 1) the subject being taught, and 2) the students being taught. Their joy is not so much in dispensing information (the teaching process), as it is in seeing students drink it in. Good teachers teach students, not curriculum!

Second, we must be creative. Teachers who do not care whether or not their students listen will not be creative. They will drone endlessly in a monotone voice, thinking, "If the students get it, fine. If they don't, too bad."

Caring, creative teachers will ask, "How can I make this interesting?" They will use illustrations, draw pictures, make rhymes, write stories, and use object lessons. Creative teachers will perk interest with provocative questions, play the Devil's advocate, be flexible, and follow rabbit trails. Wise teachers will cover less material and accomplish more in students' lives. Finally, wise teachers will involve the students in hands-on learning, realizing that students learn by doing and not just by listening. In essence, energetic teachers (with something to say) create wise students.

Final thought: Dead coals in a teacher's heart put no heat in a student's life. Burn your creative energy, and you will put a fire in your students' hearts!

PROVERBS 16:1

"The preparations of the heart in man, and the answer of the tongue, is from the Lord."

Wisdom in Heart Preparation

Thousands prepare their face each morning but forget about their heart! In Hebrew this verse reads, "The preparations of the heart belong to man, but the answer of the tongue is from the Lord." It is your responsibility to prepare your heart to face each day. God will then use your prepared heart to the greatest advantage.

Here is both a principle and a promise. The promise is that if we adequately prepare our hearts, God will give us the very words we need for every eventuality we will face this day.

The principle is that victory in our life depends on how well we prepare our hearts. If we don't prepare our hearts, God will not speak through us or use us with our students. What a fearful thought. It is imperative that we prepare our hearts.

But how do we make daily "preparations of the heart"? First, we read God's Word every morning. Second, we record what we learn about His character that day. Third, we memorize a verse for the day. Fourth, we meditate on that verse all day. Fifth, we review past "heart preparations" that we have recorded (to keep them fresh in our minds). Sixth, we pray and ask God to use His Word in our lives this day.

Final thought: Only the prepared heart can face students each morning.

Apple 83

PROVERBS 16:3

"Commit thy works unto the Lord, and thy thoughts shall be established."

Wisdom in Trusting

Worry is the sin of not trusting; but like all sin, it is far more than "wrong." It is a destructive force in life.

Worry wounds us mentally. The Greek word means "a divided mind." Charles Bridges comments, "An unsettled mind is a serious evil.… The memory is confused, the judgment undecided, the will unsteady." John Edmund Haggai adds, "Worry divides the mind between worthwhile interests and damaging thoughts.… Worry divides the understanding; therefore, convictions are shallow and changeable. Worry divides the faculty of perception; therefore, observations are faulty and even false."

Worry wounds us physically. It has been tied to heart trouble, high blood pressure, some forms of asthma, rheumatism, ulcers, cold, thyroid malfunction, migraines,…and most stomach disorders (Dr. Edward Padolsky, in *Stop Worrying and Get Well*).

Worry also wounds the soul. Sinful worry immobilizes. A worrier is afraid to make a move for fear of what might happen. Worry affects our teaching, our discipline, and our planning. Thus, Solomon writes, "Commit thy works unto the Lord, and thy thoughts (plans) shall be established."

Final thought: When we confess our sin of not trusting and commit our works to Him, the burden is lifted, the mind is eased, the thoughts are composed, and the teacher is able to manage a functional class.

When a man's ways please the Lord, he maketh even his enemies to be at peace with him."

Wisdom in Building Relationships

All relationships are based on one relationship. Peace with family, neighbors, friends, enemies, and students, is based on our relationship with the Lord.

But doesn't this run contrary to reality? How can we explain the persecution of the saints, and especially of Christ, whose ways always pleased the Lord? Charles Bridges answers this question by showing that the righteous do have enemies, but God sometimes restrains the wrath of those enemies and other times allows it because it will bring Him the most glory.

Bishop Patrick stated, "The best way for our enemies to be reconciled to us, is for us to be reconciled to God." When our ways please the Lord, parents and students, who otherwise might take offense, will have no grounds on which to act. Our very relationship with the Lord will protect us from making fleshly decisions, from making rash statements, or from using hurtful words.

Thus, it is vital that we spend quality time with the Lord and let His Word take root in our heart, so that we may abound "therein with thanksgiving" (Col. 2:7).

Final thought: "Great peace have they which love thy law: and nothing shall offend them" (Ps. 119:165). Peace in your life is proof of peace in your heart.

Apple 85

PROVERBS 16:9

"A man's heart deviseth his way: but the Lord directeth his steps."

Wisdom in Interruptions

We've often heard the maxim, "Plan your work, and work your plan." However, it is not always biblical or wise. A Christian teacher must not be tied to a plan. This seems contrary to the teacher's task of making daily lesson plans and keeping abreast of scope and sequence.

We must always be aware of the sovereignty of God in the affairs of men. Yes, it is wise to plan, but those plans must always be subjected to the disposing of God. David's shepherding was interrupted to take a lunch to his brothers. Philip was transferred from an important revival in Samaria (preaching to thousands each day), to meet with a lone eunuch in the desert (Acts 8:37–39). Paul was turned aside from a large ministry to work with a few women and a family (Acts 16:6–15, 34). Yet in each case, God used interruptions to advance His sovereign plan and to plant flourishing churches.

We need much discipline to wean ourselves from our own plans so that we may submit ourselves to God's way. The teacher who complains about constant interruptions in her schedule may be more concerned with scope and sequence than the Spirit and sovereignty. A student's question, a parent's interference, and a blown schedule should be welcomed with an eye to God's hand.

Final thought: When we think we're doing the least, God may be doing the most. Interruptions are often the hand of our Mighty God working His plan!

Wisdom in Righteous Respect

As the throne is established by righteousness, so a righteous teacher will establish his students.

Verse 12 is the third of four verses (vv. 10–13) that can be called "God's manual for kings." These verses show what God requires of kings, so that they might be a blessing to their people. If the standard is neglected, the people suffer.

The same is true of a teacher and his class. Solomon's wise handling of two women who claimed the same child is noteworthy. First Kings 3:26–28 tells us that the people "feared the king: for they saw that the wisdom of God was in him, to do judgment." As a result, Israel experienced her greatest glory under Solomon. Israel was "established."

Is this not a teacher's greatest need? If we exude the wisdom of God and the righteousness of God, our students will "fear the king," and the class will experience the glory of God! But whence do we get such wisdom and righteousness? It comes by being filled with the most righteously wise words ever spoken—the Word of God. When we are filled with and controlled by the Word, our classroom will be established.

Final thought: Respect is earned, not forced. It is earned by the righteous words, life, and wisdom of the teacher, not by demands for respect.

Apple 87

"He that handleth a matter wisely shall find good: and whoso trusteth in the Lord, happy is he."

Wisdom in Problem Solving

Every teacher is a problem solver. But not every problem solved is wisely solved. David illustrates both wisdom and foolishness in solving his problems. When faced with an invasion of the Philistines in the Valley of Rephaim, David inquired of the Lord and was rewarded with victory (2 Sam. 5:19, 23). Years later as king, rather than seek the Lord, he numbered the people to see if he had the strength to win a battle. This seemed logical enough. Does not a king count his troops to be sure he outnumbers the enemy? Yet God rebuked him for his logical act because it was motivated by fear and a lack of trust in the Lord.

When we solve problems with parents and youth, we will handle them either wisely or foolishly. The wise way is simple: turn to the Word and pray for wisdom. The foolish way is likewise simple: use human reasoning, and give culturally accepted advice.

If we really believe the Word is sufficient for every problem, then we will use it as the basis of our counsel. The Word is not meant to be learned only but also to be lived. When we counsel, "What does the Bible say?" should be our first thought.

Two truths guide the wise counselor: 1) God's Word is sufficient. Our students need no other counsel than its laws (Ps. 119:24); and 2) God's Word is supreme. We must submit to its teaching and conform our lives to its injunctions.

Final thought: The wise teacher always asks, "Is that the way the Bible says we should handle…(anger, gossip, mockery, slothfulness, disrespect, etc.)?"

"Pleasant words are as an honeycomb, sweet to the soul, and health to the bones."

Wisdom in Speech

Honey is good—and good for you—a rare combination! Generally, if it's good for you, it isn't good. If it tastes like cardboard, then it's good for you. Thus, honey is used in the Bible as the supreme symbol of the Word of God. David exclaimed, "How sweet are thy words unto my taste! Yea, sweeter than honey to my mouth" (Ps. 119:103). In another Psalm he stated that His Word was sweeter than honey and the honeycomb (Ps. 19:10). Like honey, God's Word is both good *and* good for you!

So are pleasant words. They are both "sweet to the soul, and health to the bones." Do we realize the power of our words? We can both kill and give life with the tongue. A wrong word can destroy a child for life, while pleasant words can give him spiritual health. We must be sure our words are saturated with His honey.

But what are pleasant words? When they are words of counsel, sympathy, or encouragement, they are medicinal and sweet. "But much more are the pleasant words of God both sweet and wholesome" (Charles Bridges).

If you would be satisfied and spiritually healthy, then drink deeply of God's honey. We must go to class each day, like Samson, eating our honeycomb (Judg. 14:8–9); like Jonathan, revived (1 Sam. 14:27).

Final thought: Pleasure and healing flow from the man who is full of God's Word. Let your words be "honey" for your students.

Apple 89

PROVERBS 16:24

"Pleasant words are as an honeycomb, sweet to the soul, and health to the bones."

Wisdom in Giving Hope

Not all students need to be "preached to" when they do wrong! First Thessalonians 5:14 identifies three types of problem students: The unruly (disorderly/rebellious), the feebleminded (small souled or easily discouraged); and the weak. Significantly, each type is dealt with differently. The rebellious must be warned (admonished); the feebleminded must be comforted (a word meaning to come near to and encourage); the weak must be strengthened (to prop up, stand up beside). In each case the idea of hope is very strong. Even the word *warn* is a Greek word that generally means to counsel with biblical instruction. The last two verbs (*comfort* and *support*) both imply the act of encouragement. Youth who are easily discouraged especially need hope. Berating them for their failure may well doom them to further failure. Sin and failure kills the spirit of many.

It is our job to be "health to the bones" even when they have committed the vilest of sins! When Jesus met the woman taken in adultery, He did not berate her (though her sin was grievous) but rather told her that He did not accuse her and to "go and sin no more." That statement offered hope and health.

Final thought: Use pleasant words when dealing with defeated youth. You may well be the means of saving them from destruction.

"There is a way that seemeth right unto a man, but the end thereof are the ways of death."

Wisdom in Dealing with Naïvete and Delusion

Youth, like all of us, have sinful natures. But unlike adults, childhood naïvete magnifies their problem. Their sin nature gives them a desire for wrong, and their lack of knowledge and understanding greases the way.

Our job is to show students that what may seem right might actually lead to death. We must realize that "All the ways of a man are clean in his own eyes" (Prov. 16:2). Even the persecutors of believers think they are doing God service (John 16:2). Lying seems better than truth when it will help us escape trouble. Cheating seems better than making a bad grade and disappointing our parents! All our sin *seems* to be so good and beneficial. "But the end thereof are the ways of death."

Teachers must continually remind youth of the consequences of evil. Use biblical illustrations: David's sin with Bathsheba seemed right to David, but it cost him his son. Keeping the best of the sheep to sacrifice to God seemed to be so right to Saul, but it cost him his throne. Scriptures are full of such illustrations. Further, use current events to remind youth that what seems right may destroy a life. (A night of drinking leads to death, etc. Your newspapers are full of such information.)

Final thought: Immaturity seldom looks beyond the present. Instill in teens the fear of the Lord and the fear of sin!

Apple 91

PROVERBS 16:27

"An ungodly man diggeth up evil: and in his lips there is as a burning fire."

Wisdom in Dealing with Discordant Youth

Some youth seem hell–bent on destruction. If they can't find anything to destroy, they will dig something up. It may be something that happened two years earlier. It may be a complete lie. Either way, they will find it and make it an issue. How do we deal with such discord in our class?

First, we should use the language of the Bible in describing this sin. Remind offenders that God calls a man who does such a thing, ungodly, or (simply put) not like God. When God forgives, He forgets. He promises, "Your sins and iniquities will I remember no more" (Heb. 8:12). Thus, digging up past (or even present) sin is un–godlike. The word translated *ungodly* is, if possible, even stronger than *fool* says one commentary. Those who dig up past sin are like grave robbers. They bring up dead issues and use them to start a burning fire. Their lips delight in reminding others of their past failures.

Second, we must show them the origin of their discordant ways. The burning fire in their lips is set on fire of hell. Satan is the slayer of men, and he often uses our tongues as his weapon! Thus, James says that the tongue that sows discord is born in hell (James 3:6). Not a pleasant description.

Final thought: Face falsehood, gossip, and divisive speech with the True Word. Use Scripture to bring conviction, and douse the fire of hell.

PROVERBS 16:28

"A froward man soweth strife: and a whisperer separateth chief friends."

Wisdom in Dealing with Divisive Youth

Today's devotional continues the thought from yesterday. Both verses address divisive speech. This verse focuses on the consequences of divisive speech. It can destroy the closest relationship, especially when the offender intends to spread strife.

Again, note God's language in describing the slanderer. Divisive speech is characteristic of the froward. This word can be translated "perverse," "malicious," or "crooked." It is connected with lying or fraudulent speech. The idea behind the word is to change or twist a fact so that it appears to mean something else entirely. It is a favorite trick of the gossip or the slanderer. Its intention is to sow strife. For a person to be characterized as froward is to say they are themselves crooked and fraudulent.

The word *whisperer* means "to roll to pieces." Thus, the whisperer will not let a thing die! He will continue to bring it up until he has at last turned friend against friend.

We must be careful that we identify such behavior in our class and show youth what God thinks of this practice. Further, we must be certain that we do not practice it in our church, in our class, or among our fellow-workers.

Final thought: Those who bend truth are themselves bent (crooked)!

Apple 93

PROVERBS 16:32

"He that is slow to anger is better than the mighty; and he that ruleth his spirit than he that taketh a city."

Wisdom in Self–Control

He who captures a city can lose it to a stronger foe. Self–control, however, can never be conquered. Looking at this verse in reverse we realize that losing one's temper defeats a man. We always lose when we lose control.

Those who cannot control their spirit cannot control their class. Some seek to control their class by shouting, demanding, and threatening. Others control their class by controlling themselves. Far more "mighty" is the latter. Charles Bridges put it this way: "Instead of having rule over their spirit, they are captives, not conquerors."

The word translated *slow to anger* is actually the Hebrew for "long–nosed." It is in contrast to the short breathing and snorting of an angry man. The "short–nosed" feel they have good reason to be angry (Jonah, for example). Teachers may feel the same justification toward a disobedient student—it's a disgrace to put up with wrong! Thus, they excuse their temper as "righteous indignation."

But should a Christian teacher act this way? James commands us to bridle our tongue and so check our passions. Paul reminds us to "let all bitterness, and wrath, and anger...be put away from you, with all malice" (Eph. 4:31).

Final thought: "Be not many masters [teachers], knowing that we shall receive the greater condemnation" (James 3:1).

"Whoso mocketh the poor reproacheth his Maker: and he that is glad at calamities shall not be unpunished."

Wisdom in Showing Respect

Youth are the world's worst at respecting the feelings of others. In their naïvete they laugh and scoff when someone fails or makes a dumb remark. They laugh at the out–of–style dress of the poor, or they scoff at the awkwardness of the unathletic child.

Much more do they enjoy the problems and punishment of their enemies. Though most of us would never admit it, our selfish spirit may inwardly laugh at the news that our enemy has fallen, yet even this is sin.

A teacher's job is to teach students to respect others—even their enemies—regardless of their talent, appearance, dress, race, or position in life. How do we do this?

First, use Scripture. Always counsel with Scripture as the authority. Use this verse to teach respect. Other verses include Proverbs 24:17, 18; Psalm 35:11–14; and Romans 12:20–21.

Second, remind them that we are all created in the image of God. Thus, to mock God's image is a sin of the deepest dye (Gen. 9:6)!

Final thought: Teach your class to pray for each other by name, rather than mock each other in shame.

Apple 95

PROVERBS 17:17

"A friend loveth at all times, and a brother is born for adversity."

Wisdom in Friendship

Teachers must be more than instructors. They must be friends to their students. Some circles propose that teachers should stay at arm's length from their students so as to maintain proper respect. This, however, is not what the Bible teaches. Christ came down from heaven to live among men, to call out a people for His name, and to call them friends (John 15:14–15). Did they have less respect for Him as He lived among them? No. They had more respect for Him the closer they got to Him!

If we are genuine followers of the Lamb, we will get close to our students. We will get involved in their personal lives and counsel them. This will not lessen their respect but rather enhance it! The closer students get to us, the closer they get to the Lamb, and the more respect they will have for both!

How does one treat a friend who has disobeyed? He still loves him ("A friend loveth at all times"). But, he also will confront his friend with his sin. Thus, "a brother is born for adversity." Part of friendship is confronting our students with their failures in a kind way and showing them biblical steps to overcome it.

Final thought: Come down from your authority perch and mingle with your students, so that you can be a trusted friend in their times of adversity.

Wisdom in Outlook

A merry heart is here contrasted with a broken spirit. While God wants us to have a broken and contrite heart (Ps. 51:17) in regard to our sin, he does not want us to have a despondent and negative spirit. The contrast in this verse is in regards to one's attitude and outlook in life. We are to be happy, excited, positive, and encouraging. It is not fitting that a child of a victorious God should live in despair and gloom. We have every reason to rejoice, yet some believers live in the dark and dank cave of despair and gloom.

Beware the broken spirit! It looks at the dark side and broods over circumstances. It is quick to complain and slow to smile and laugh. And it will dry up the bones. Physically, a negative spirit will drain our energy, sap our strength, and rob us of vitality and life.

Further, a negative outlook will dry up our spiritual vitality because we fail to see the power and majesty of God. We lose the joy of seeing answered prayer. Instead of praise, our tongue complains. And what are the results? Not only are we worse off, but so is our class. God dies in their souls. Christianity shrivels to an ancient creed to be slavishly memorized and served.

Final thought: You can be a saving medicine or a somber mortician to your class. Look up! Gather in His sunshine, and show His healing power to your class.

Apple 97

PROVERBS 18:1

"Through desire a man, having separated himself, seeketh and intermeddleth with all wisdom."

Wisdom in Humility

This verse is often misunderstood. On the surface it seems to be saying that a man that wants wisdom should seek it in solitude. However, that is not really what the verse means. Far from encouraging solitude, this verse actually condemns the schismatic attitude of the man that goes his own way. A better way to understand this verse is "a divisive man seeks an opportunity for a quarrel; he rails against all sound policy" (*The New American Commentary*).

I remember hearing a pastor tell the story of a man in his church who was very contrary. He finally told the man, "I believe that if the deacons passed a resolution that the sky was blue, you'd disagree with that too!" Some people are never happy unless they are being contrary. Some teachers enjoy irritating the administration over inconsequential things.

A divisive teacher is one that looks for opportunities to quarrel. He or she is proud. That's the bottom line. This person will disagree with sound policy just because they want to disagree. Are you that teacher? Do you have a conflict with the administration right now? Is it because you are a divisive person? You may claim that your disagreement is over principle. I've heard it said that "many an angry man has masqueraded as a righteous crusader." Many a divisive teacher has masqueraded this way as well.

Final thought: Sometimes we show our wisdom by what we don't say.

Wisdom in Trusting

So often in times of trial we trust our own machinations. Solomon mentions the rich man in the following verse and announces that his wealth is his strong city and like a high wall in his own imagination. We seek to find our own ways to extricate ourselves from the burning furnaces of life (Eccles. 7:29).

But the righteous have found a better way—the strong tower of God's name. When the righteous face impossible trials, rather than trust their own worry, fret, preoccupations, and devices, they have learned to call on the name of the Lord. They run into it and are safe. They trust Him rather than their own wits. They rest. They pray. They reflect on His character.

Psalm 9:10 says, "And they that know thy name will put their trust in thee: for thou, Lord, hast not forsaken them that seek thee." He is El–Shaddai (the all–sufficient God who will supply all I need). He is El–Elyon (most high—able to see all and do far more than I could even think). He is YHWH (Jehovah/Lord—the one in total control). Why should I fight my problems? I will instead run to my strong tower and let Him, who is all in all, fight them for me.

Final thought: Read Psalm 91 and note the psalmist's wisdom in trusting.

Apple 99

PROVERBS 18:13

"He that answereth a matter before he heareth it, it is folly and shame unto him."

Wisdom in Reserving Judgment

The foolish person jumps to conclusions, but when he is proven wrong, then he is shamed. We know this, yet how often do we put on our jumping shoes? Sadly, we *react* rather than act. Job's friend, Elihu, considerately restrained himself until he had thoroughly heard the matter (Job 32:4, 10, 11). Better by far that we gather information before we come to conclusions.

To reserve judgment is to show wisdom, but it is also a display of humility. Those who quickly judge a matter pride themselves in their astute judgment. They don't need facts because their intuition is so iron-clad that they know the answer before they hear the question! Potiphar imprisoned Joseph because he failed to get the facts. He let his jealousy and wrath interfere with sound judgment. Yet our omniscient God examined Adam before He pronounced judgment. He came down to see Babel and Sodom prior to their destruction. Does our knowledge exceed the All-Wise and Knowing Savior? We quickly judge our students, yet we have never visited their homes. We snap at them, but we do not know that they have a physical problem or that other circumstances are at work. Better that (in humility) we confess we are not all-wise and gather the facts before we react.

Final thought: He who is wise does not trust his eyes!

PROVERBS 18:17

"He that is first in his own cause seemeth just; but his neighbour cometh and searcheth him."

Wisdom in Listening

This passage parallels yesterday's. He who is wise does not trust his eyes, but neither does he trust his ears. Have you noticed that there are always two sides to a story? The first sounds so right—so true—that surely this person is in the right and the other wrong. Yet if we would delay our judgment until we heard the other side, we would realize that everything is not black and white. How often has a tale of an uncaring parent or a broken home roused our sympathy? But a close look at the other side of the story revealed the error of a hasty, one-sided judgment. Wisdom has taught us to see both sides.

Is it not also true that we cannot see our own problems with perfect accuracy? Where our own name or credit is concerned, our argument "seemeth just." We rush in first with our own tale. We rationalize and reason ourselves righteous. But according to this proverb, the first tale is good until the second is heard. Our friend comes, examines us, exposes our failure, and puts us to shame. Saul convinced himself that he was right in sparing the best of the sheep—until his "neighbor" came and exposed his sin. In our own case we should guard against a self-justifying spirit.

Final thought: Listen carefully to both sides of a case—especially when you are one of the sides!

Apple 101

PROVERBS 18:24

"A man that hath friends must shew himself friendly: and there is a friend that sticketh closer than a brother."

Wisdom in Depending on Friends

This verse has proven difficult for translators. The word translated *must show himself friendly* is actually a single word that has two meanings: "to break in pieces/to shatter" or "to shout in triumph." Most scholars thus interpret the first half of the verse to say, "A man of many friends shouts in triumph" (that is, he proudly boasts of how popular he is), or "A man of many friends will come to ruin" (that is, he will have more heartaches because "friends" often turn against us). If either of these translations is accurate, then the first half of the verse is in contrast to the latter half, which states that there is a friend who will never let us down. In other words, a true friend is a rare and treasured jewel.

Regardless of the translation problems, the verse teaches that it is better to have one true friend than a multitude of sycophants, who will turn on us when they disagree with our actions. And often it is true that those who butter you up the most are those who will as quickly become your enemy. Thus, we must be careful of our friends. Choose them wisely.

Finally, a wise teacher will trust in his One True Friend (the Lord Jesus Christ) more than in a hundred human friends. Why? Mankind is subject to selfishness and is thus prone to forsake us in our time of deepest need. Even our best friend may disappoint us in time of trouble. But Christ will never disappoint.

Final thought: Be a true friend to your students—even when they fail!

"The foolishness of man perverteth his way: and his heart fretteth against the Lord."

Wisdom in Confronting Sin

It's man's nature to sin—and to blame God for it. Yet it is his own foolishness that perverts his way. Here we see a man blaming God for his own perversion ("his heart fretteth against the Lord"). He might say, "It's not my fault that I have these strong desires. I can't help it. God made me this way." Such is the thinking of modern society. Charles Manson once remarked that he did no wrong in the Sharon Tate murders because "he felt like it." Surely, if he felt like it, God must have given him those desires (so he tragically reasoned)!

While we see the folly of such a statement, do not our students (and their parents) often say essentially the same thing? "I couldn't help it. So and so made me do it." "It's the crowd she was with." Such statements dodge the issue of man's own foolishness perverting his way. The wise teacher will help students take responsibility for their own sin and show them what God says about it in the Bible. We call it "stretching the truth," but the Bible calls it lying. It isn't "cheating;" it's stealing. We need to use biblical terminology for sin. We need for students to confess, "I have sinned," "I have disobeyed God's Word," "I have lied," etc.

Further, we must show them that they *could* help it! First Corinthians 10:13 plainly states, "…but God is faithful, who will not suffer you to be tempted above that ye are able; but will with the temptation also make a way to escape…."

Final thought: Help youth face their sinfulness squarely, accept the blame, name it for what it really is, and confess it.

Apple 103

PROVERBS 19:5

"A false witness shall not be unpunished, and he that speaketh lies shall not escape."

Wisdom in Dealing with Lies

How big can a lie become? "It's only a little fib," someone says. "It's just a white lie." "I was only joking." These are but a few of the cover-ups for what God calls lying. If a truthful witness delivereth souls (Prov. 14:25), a false witness destroys them. Satan's lie brought about the fall of all mankind, and many are the illustrations in the Bible of the destructive force of a lie.

Charles Bridges stated:

"Strict attention to truth forms a primary point in Christian education. The boundary line must never be trifled with. Not even a child can pass it without paying a price. It will soon lose its respect, if it isn't reverenced at any cost and under all circumstances. A child must never be allowed to play with a lie. It must constantly be pressed upon him that anything less than truth is a lie. Even if no one is deceived by it, a habit is fostered, and we can't tell how big it will actually become."

Small white lies grow into larger ones. Soon, respect for truth is lost. Lying will eventually banish the fear of being under oath. It will be excused to cover up sin. It will ultimately be used to destroy a life! This happens by degrees, and it begins in the home and in the classroom.

Final thought: Do not allow lying in your classroom. Call your students on it and chasten them while there is hope!

P R O V E R B S   1 9 : 1 1

"The discretion of a man deferreth his anger; and it is his glory to pass over a transgression."

Wisdom in Personal Attacks

When others sin, it is right to confront them in a spirit of meekness. However, when one sins against us, it is often best to let it pass! The discrete man (literally, man of insight, intelligence) will delay his anger. He will *pass over* (literally, cover) sins against him.

The proud respond another way. The pride of man will glow white–hot when someone dares to offend him. He will not hold his anger but will be quick to lash out and reveal his ego!

Someone has called anger "temporary madness." We yield to angry outbursts or act impulsively because we are not guarded by humility. Men are especially prone to this temptation. They are likely to feel that overlooking an offense shows a lack of courage and manhood. But Solomon declares the ability to bear offense graciously to be a strength, rather than a weakness. And is this not showing the Spirit of Christ who as "a sheep before her shearers is dumb, so he openeth not his mouth" (Isa. 53:7). Yet was there ever one that was manlier than our Lord?

No, it isn't good character and strength that causes us to lash out at others; it is poor character and weakness that does so. And in so doing, we lose the respect of those we teach or lead.

Final thought: A closed mouth and a meek spirit can glorify God more than a thousand words!

Apple 105

PROVERBS 19:12

"The king's wrath is as the roaring of a lion; but his favour is as dew upon the grass."

Wisdom in Leadership

Everything a king does is magnified in the eyes of men. His anger is much hotter, his failures much more grievous, and his kindness far more glorious than any other in the kingdom. Why? He is the leader. He is in the spotlight. His subjects' lives are tied to his actions, motives, and character. In this way the king of the field is like the king of the forest. The prophet Amos asks, "The lion hath roared, who will not fear?" (Amos 3:8). The animals of the forest run in every direction at the sound. So it is with all leaders. So it will be in a teacher's class.

A teacher can be a lion, or she can be as dew upon the grass! She can lead her class two ways: by fear or by favor! Better it is that she learn the power of dew than the power of the lion. The lion frightens and causes death and dread. The tiny dew refreshes and brings life and vigor.

What is the dew that refreshes a class? In this instance it is called the favor of the king. The Hebrew means "that which is pleasing or acceptable." *Dew* is that which encourages and nourishes your class. It is kindness and words of affirmation. Are you the refreshing dew or the roaring lion to your students? One tears down, while the other builds up!

Final thought: The lion rules the forest, roaring to and fro, while the dew, though unnoticed, makes the forest grow!

PROVERBS 19:15
"Slothfulness casteth into a deep sleep; and an idle soul shall suffer hunger."

Wisdom in Fervency

If a lazy teacher is bad, a lazy Christian teacher is worse! We have every reason to be fervent in spirit because we serve the Lord God—the King of Kings and Lord of Lords! Paul reminds believers that we must not be "slothful in business" but rather be "fervent in spirit; serving the Lord" (Rom. 12:11).

A lazy teacher is slovenly in preparation and in presentation. He loads his students with homework because he doesn't have the discipline to cover the material in class! His lack of preparation leads to a lack of creativity in presentation. His lack of energy saps his enthusiasm, and he puts his students to sleep. "Slothfulness casteth into a deep sleep." A lazy voice (monotone, without energy or enthusiasm) is like the droning of a plane. Soon the passengers are nodding off, yet this same teacher will upbraid the students for their inattentiveness.

A lazy teacher is slovenly in correction and in counsel. He would rather give demerits and rebuke than counsel and encouragement. It takes energy and time to counsel students and help them overcome their problems, so he carelessly hands out demerits and lashes with his tongue.

Final thought: Check your energy level. Are you excited about God? Are you fervently serving the Lord? Are you slothful in teaching?

Apple 107

PROVERBS 19:20

"Hear counsel, and receive instruction, that thou mayest be wise in thy latter end."

Wisdom in Listening, Part 1

This verse cuts several ways. First, it applies to you as the counselee. Second, it applies to your students. Third, it applies to you as the counselor.

As the counselee, we must be ready to listen and learn. We do make mistakes! Teachers do mishandle situations, and they do not know all the answers. But pride is the chief enemy of learning and accepting instruction. "Who are they to teach me? What do they know more than me?" These are the words of pride, and they block the door to future wisdom.

Second, our students must learn to listen, and they need to be reminded constantly. Have them memorize and quote this verse in class when they do not pay attention. Admonish inattentiveness with Scripture. Solomon tells us in Ecclesiastes 11:10 that "childhood and youth are vanity." That is, most youth waste their time. Present gratification is their main object with little regard for the future. In sarcasm Solomon tells them to "walk in the ways of thine heart, and in the sight of thine eyes" (Eccles. 11:9). In other words, "Don't listen; go happily on your way!" Then he adds "But know thou, that for all these things God will bring thee into judgment."

Final thought: Use Scripture to teach attentiveness. If they will not listen to God, they will not listen to you!

PROVERBS 19:20

"Hear counsel, and receive instruction, that thou mayest be wise in thy latter end."

Wisdom in Listening, Part 2

Yesterday we discussed two ways this verse may be applied: to you as the counselee and to your students. There is a third way you must apply this verse: to you as a counselor.

It is as important for the teacher to listen to the students as it is for the students to listen to the teacher. Listening cuts both ways. The counselor who will not listen is set on pride. He assumes he has all the answers. However, if we do not listen carefully, we may miss the most vital direction for our counsel. Essentially, a teacher is in the business of communication, and one half of communication is listening. Proverbs 18:13 reminds us, "He that answereth a matter before he heareth it, it is folly and shame unto him." Often our students tell us things that we do not even hear. We have already made up our minds. We have already judged them to be rebellious, disobedient, lazy, or incompetent. Yet we have not carefully listened to what is in their hearts. James admonishes us, "Let every man be swift to hear, slow to speak, slow to wrath" (James 1:19).

Good counselors are good listeners. They ask questions and listen carefully to the answers. They want to know what is in the heart.

Final thought: Turn your ears on before you engage your mouth.

Apple 109

PROVERBS 19:21

"There are many devices in a man's heart; nevertheless the counsel of the Lord, that shall stand."

Wisdom in Counsel

Do you believe in the sufficiency of the Word? Do you practice it? This verse contrasts the devices of a man and the counsel of the Lord. Too often we depend on our own devices rather than the Word. We entice youth to obey (or we force them to obey) rather than show them the clear teaching of God's Word and challenge them to do what it says!

A *device* is a manipulative means of affecting behavior apart from the Word. For example, the parents of a rebellious teen at first used human devices to keep their child away from her ungodly friends. However, they soon realized the problem hadn't been solved. She couldn't see her friends, but her heart wasn't changed. They used external means to deal with an internal problem. Upon seeking biblical counsel, the teenager was saved and began a process of spiritual growth. Her parents realized that it was better to use the Word to affect her heart than to manipulate her to do what was right.

Devices may change behavior, but only God's Word can change the heart! Children must be shown which verses of Scripture they are disobeying and which commands of God they must obey.

Final thought: Only correction sourced in God's Word will last.

P R O V E R B S   1 9 : 2 2

"The desire of a man is his kindness: and a poor man is better than a liar."

Wisdom in Kind Truthfulness

Kindness and truth make the perfect couple! To be a kind liar is to be a deadly deceiver. To be an unkind judge is to be an ogre. Jesus stood for truth but still forgave the repentant. He denounced arrogance, pretense, and pride, but forgave the woman taken in adultery, fed the hungry, gave sight to the blind, wept over Jerusalem, and gave his life a ransom for many.

While it is important to "speak the truth," we must ever do so "in love" (Eph. 4:15). Balancing truth with love may be the most difficult of all Christian exercises, yet God's Word requires both. You must never lie by glossing over a sin—whether it is in your life or that of your students. It is better to be poor than to fail to confront sin. Second Timothy 3:16 reveals that the Bible is profitable for four things— one of them being reproof. This word means to bring a person under conviction. Thus, the Word is to be used wisely and kindly in our classrooms to show youth that they are guilty. Only this "kind confrontation" with the Word will bring conviction for sin and will cause both parents and youth to appreciate you even more for loving them enough to use Scripture to illuminate their sin.

Final thought: The most attractive teachers are those who kindly and consistently use Scripture to confront sin in their students' lives!

Apple 111

PROVERBS 19:24

"A slothful man hideth his hand in his bosom, and will not so much as bring it to his mouth again."

Wisdom in the Daily Disciplines

Laziness affects more than one's job. It also affects one's spiritual growth. So debilitating is laziness that the slothful will not even provide for his noon meal! He would rather be hungry than use his energy to prepare a meal.

While we may think such laziness is inexcusable, does this not illustrate our spiritual laziness? Spiritual growth requires daily discipline and industry. Prayer is work. Daily devotions are a struggle. These come easy to no one, but the spiritually lazy will especially suffer. Lethargy will stop our hand from reaching out to partake of the daily bread.

We can wish to live a fruitful life of prayer and devotions yet fail to do so because of spiritual slothfulness. How sad at the end to "remember that all this was wished, yes, even resolved; yet not a bit of it accomplished" (Bridges).

Do you wish to have a better prayer life, a deeper devotional life, a deeper intimacy with God? What keeps you from it? Is it the most deadly of sins—spiritual lethargy?

When prayer is cold and heartless, pray more. When God's Word is dry and meaningless, meditate more. Form habits of early energy. Turn wishing into action. Cultivate bodily activity.

Final thought: Spiritual laziness is a poison that only discipline can assuage!

Wisdom in Education

Christian education finds its *raison d'être* in this verse! Children are commanded to cease listening to those philosophies that hinder obedience to the Word of God. The same words came from Christ, "Beware of false prophets" (Matt. 7:15), and "Take heed what ye hear" (Mark 4:24). Not all instruction is truth. And that which is not truth is not true education! Worse, that which is not truth will lead youth astray and cause them to "err from the words of knowledge."

If secular education causes youth to err from the words of knowledge, then Christian education exists to enable youth to follow the words of knowledge!

Thus, only that education which confronts youth with the very words of Scripture is truly Christian. It is not enough to tell students that they should not lie or that they should not steal or criticize. Even responsible members of secular society tell them that. Instead, we must show them from the words of knowledge that they must replace lying with truth, replace stealing with labor, and replace gossip with wholesome words. When youth err from the words of knowledge, we must use the words of knowledge to reprove them of their sin. This is the heart of Christian education.

Final thought: Christian educators are not "Christianly educating" if they are not using the very words of knowledge to convict, correct, and instruct in righteous living (2 Tim. 3:16).

Apple 113

PROVERBS 20:5

"Counsel in the heart of man is like deep water; but a man of understanding will draw it out."

Wisdom in Transparency

What is at the bottom of a child's heart is difficult to discover, but a wise teacher will take the time to draw it out. Sadly, we are often too busy "educating" to know our students. They may have deep scars from a dysfunctional home. They may have root sin problems that lead to habitual sin patterns. But instead of taking the time to draw out the deeper problem, we only attack the surface problem. In essence we place band–aids on boils!

Drawing out what a child really thinks requires four elements: time, understanding, a listening ear, and personal transparency. A teacher must take time at lunch, during class breaks, and other informal moments to get to know her students. She must ask questions, probe, and allow the student to be transparent without judging or reacting to the words that come from the depths.

But, if we are to draw out the depths of a child's heart, we must be willing to reveal the depths of our own heart to our students. Only those teachers who are transparent themselves will have transparent students. How gifted are you at sharing your frailties, failures, burdens, wishes, heartaches, and joys with your students?

Final thought: Share the depths of your heart if you would plumb the depths of your students' hearts.

Wisdom in a Look

An admired leader needs but to look on the guilty to dispel their evil, but a weaker man is not so. God often leads with the simple look of His eye! "The foolish shall not stand in thy sight" (Ps. 5:5). "His eyes behold, his eyelids try the children of men" (Ps. 11:4). "He ruleth by his power forever, his eyes behold the nations" (Ps. 66:7).

Further, the Lord reminds David, "I will guide thee with mine eye" (Ps. 32:8). Such is the power of a righteous leader! The power, however, is not in the eye but in the admiration and love of the person behind the eye.

A godly, beloved parent or teacher can likewise stop many a misdeed with a simple look! When children admire their teacher, a look may serve as correction better than words. Loud words and harsh threatening are the tools of the weak. Jesus was so gentle that "a bruised reed shall he not break, and smoking flax shall he not quench" (Matt. 12:20). Such is the power of a righteous life! Do youth so admire your character that you can lead with a look?

Final thought: The ability to govern with the eyes as easily as with the mouth is the true test of godly leadership!

Apple 115

PROVERBS 20:11

"Even a child is known by his doings, whether his work be pure, and whether it be right."

Wisdom in Observation

A wise teacher is an observing teacher. She takes note of her students' habits, tempers, and deeds. Often the child will tell what the man will be. No teacher will pass over little faults. If a child is deceitful, quarrelsome, stubborn, or selfish, it must be wisely dealt with from the Word. Children must be led to see the ugly future of their early sin.

First, a teacher should list her children separately and beside each name list areas where the child needs to grow.

Second, the teacher should pray for the child in each of these specific areas. Our prayer should be two–fold: that God would do a work in his heart and life to change the student and that we would have wisdom in dealing with the child from Scripture in each of these areas.

Third, use specific Scripture with each student to help him see his sin and provide him with steps to overcome it.

Fourth, exercise patience, realizing that oak trees don't grow overnight! Augustine's mother had a difficult time while he was young. Later she remarked, "It is impossible that the child of so many prayers could ever perish."

Final thought: Observing and correcting students' lives is no easy task, but Christian teachers (disciplers) teach for just this purpose!

PROVERBS 20:21

"An inheritance may be gotten hastily at the beginning; but the end thereof shall not be blessed."

Wisdom in Taking Our Time

The old adage "haste makes waste" has a biblical basis! As a general principle, that which comes easily or instantly vanishes just as soon. Lasting things generally require time and pain to develop. Solomon's inheritance that is gotten hastily is obviously that which is gotten by dishonest, manipulative, or selfish means. Its end will not be blessed.

Let this be a warning in the training of youth. David calls youth "a heritage (inheritance) of the Lord" (Ps. 127:3). But such an inheritance is not gained in a day, or even a semester. Rather, true godliness is developed through the slow process of progressive sanctification, and it is the product of years of scriptural indoctrination and obedience to the Word. Manipulation, coercion, and a system of regimented rules may give the illusion of godliness, but "the end thereof shall not be blessed."

It is your mission to begin the process of spiritual growth. You can only do this as you emphasize both the supremacy and the sufficiency of God's Word in the hearts and lives of your students. Only as you confront every area of their lives with the question, "What does the Bible say?" will the seeds of future godliness be sown.

Final thought: Don't give up! The blessings of the future are sown in the present, and tomorrow's godly leaders often come from the bottom of the class!

Apple 117

PROVERBS 20:30

"The blueness of a wound cleanseth away evil: so do stripes the inward parts of the belly."

Wisdom in Appropriate Discipline

Punishment is the Lord's way of bringing pain to the flesh in order to bring profit to the spirit. God's concern is always for the "inward parts." The point of the verse (difficult to accurately translate into proper English), however, seems to be that there are "different strokes for different folks" but always to one end—development of the inner man! The Complete Biblical Library suggests, "The wise understand the need to correct those who are in their care, and to do so thoughtfully, applying the right form of rebuke at the appropriate time" (25:11f).

First Thessalonians 5:14 distinguishes between those who are *unruly, feebleminded,* and *weak.* Each requires a different stroke! The unruly must be *warned* (a Greek word that implies confronting the sinner with Scripture), the feebleminded must be *comforted* (encouraged), and the weak must be *supported.* Thus, godly discipline requires discernment, appropriate action, and proper motive.

To *discern,* we must be so transparent with youth that they are transparent with us! We must see the mind and heart beyond the action. Only then can we apply *appropriate discipline* (whether scriptural confrontation, encouragement, or biblical steps for victory). The *proper motive* is to develop the "inward parts," rather than simply to effect outward change.

Final thought: Without proper medication, wounds are not healed; and without appropriate correction, character is not developed.

"The king's heart is in the hand of the Lord, as the rivers of water: he turneth it whithersoever he will."

Wisdom in Making an Appeal

What do we do when we disagree with administrative policies or when we want to do something that we think would benefit us (or our students), but the administration or board does not agree? We follow the advice given in this verse.

First, we must recognize that the God who formed the rivers and changes their course as He wills also holds the hearts of those for whom we work in the palm of His hand. He can as easily change the minds of the authorities in our lives as He can change the flow of a mighty river.

Next, armed with that understanding, we go to the King of Kings and ask Him to change the heart of our "king." As we pray, we must also submit ourselves to accept the outcome, whatever it may be. Keep in mind that God works in the heart of the obstinate, the unsaved, and the stubborn as easily as he works in the heart of the humble, godly leader. No matter how impossible a situation may seem, God is able to change the heart of the king.

Finally, appeal to the authority—but only when you have a well thought–through (and prayed–through) plan to present and a willingness to accept the decision (no matter what it is) as from the Lord.

Final thought: God can also change your heart and make it willing to accept a contrary decision from your authority.

Apple 119

PROVERBS 21:5

"The thoughts of the diligent tend only to plenteousness; but of every one that is hasty only to want."

Wisdom in Plodding

The tortoise wins again. Usually the diligent is contrasted with the lazy. But here, the diligent is contrasted with the hasty. That is, the plodding, thinking, planning, patient, hard–working man makes progress by degrees and ultimately ends up ahead. The hasty are often characterized by undisciplined impulse. They rush ahead without thinking. The mouth moves before the mind is engaged. The hand acts before the heart controls. They are more concerned with covering all the material, than with making sure the students understand.

A wise man had this advice for those he saw in a hurry to get things done "Slow down a little, so we can get this job done sooner!" A diligent teacher may cover less material but accomplish more in her students' hearts.

The problem with haste in our life is that we have no time for prayer. The problem with haste in the classroom is that we have little time for comprehension and counsel. The problem with haste in our decisions is that we run ahead of God. The Lord takes His time. He operates from the perspective of eternity, while we operate from the perspective of 70 years! The God of Eternity is our employer, and we must operate by His time card!

Final thought: Haste may waste a heart. In your haste to cover the material, don't rush past an opportunity to reach your students' hearts!

Wisdom in Controlling Anger

Nothing is as destructive as a quarrelling, angry spouse—or teacher. Solomon feels so strongly about it that he mentions it again in 21:9, 25:4, and 26:21. An uncontrolled temper may drive a spouse out of the house! Contentious, nagging people can so destroy the peace that the goal becomes singular—escape from their presence.

This principle is as applicable to the school as to the home. A teacher with uncontrolled anger will drive his class to despair. Escape becomes the only hope for the students. How do they escape? They clam up. As a turtle retreats into his shell, so students find shelter in silence. The result is an unapproachable and ineffective teacher. As Cain's anger led to the murder of Abel, so our anger may kill the transparency of open communication in our class.

The problem with anger is that everyone but the guilty can see it. It is so much a part of his character that what he calls "raising my voice a bit" is in reality screaming or shouting. What he calls "telling the truth" is in reality bludgeoning others with hurtful words that cut to the soul.

Final thought: Check your "anger barometer." Do your students openly share their hurts, problems, and prayer requests with you, or do they seek out others? Do they flock around you, or do they remain aloof?

Apple 121

PROVERBS 21:21

"He that followeth after righteousness and mercy findeth life, righteousness, and honour."

Wisdom in Righteous Pursuits

Twenty–first century life is so fast that even the most committed Christian often struggles with vain priorities. Solomon wrote an entire book on the vanity of wrong pursuits. He called it chasing the wind (Eccles. 5:16).

If mature adults battle with such vanities, our youth struggle all the more. Satan has them chasing soap bubbles. And sadly, they are often led in their empty pursuit by Christian parents and teachers who are also chasing the wind! How do we make sure our students do not get caught up in such vain pursuits?

First, we must *make sure our own pursuits are righteous*. Are we most animated when we talk about our devotions, our Lord, and the Word, or when we speak of entertainment, sports, our hobbies, or other pursuits?

Second, we must *make sure our righteous pursuits are contagious*. This is accomplished by the verbal, enthusiastic sharing of the treasures we glean from our devotions. Talk excitedly about your relationship to the Lord each day.

Finally, *share illustrations of the emptiness of chasing the wind*. Your newspapers abound with stories of entertainers who chased the wind only to find death from drugs, AIDS, or suicide.

Final thought: Our hunger for righteousness must be so contagious that our students become Son–chasers rather than wind–chasers.

PROVERBS 21:31

"The horse is prepared against the day of battle: but safety is of the Lord."

Wisdom in Preparation

Of course teachers know about lesson preparation. It is a daily chore for the new teacher but old hat for those who have taught the same curriculum for years. It is an important part of teaching.

However, do we prepare as we should? One aspect of lesson preparation that often goes unnoticed is prayer. Yet it is probably the most important aspect of lesson preparation. How often do I find myself spending hours in sermon preparation—doing research, word studies, outlining, meditating, and writing—only to realize that I have spent just a few minutes in actual prayer!

The last phrase of Proverbs 21:31 reminds us that all our preparation is in vain if the Lord is not involved. For "safety is of the Lord." All of our burdens for youth, our words, our urging, our counseling, and our teaching are in vain unless the Lord is at work! He is the One whose power must be invoked.

Each day we go forth to battle with a prepared horse (our lesson preparation), but have we spent time with the Lord of the battle? Do we depend on our years of experience, our lesson preparation, and our extensive skills to lead us in battle, or do we go forth with trembling and in the power of the Lord?

Final thought: Our most effective lesson preparation is done on our knees!

Apple 123

PROVERBS 22:2

"The rich and poor meet together: the Lord is the maker of them all.

Wisdom in Accepting Others

Students struggle with wrong values. In elementary school name–calling and insults are not uncommon. The handicapped, the slow–learner, and the less developed are the butt of cruel jokes. In high school the athletic, the best look-ing, or the best dressed often lead the popularity parade. Even teachers are often guilty of favoring the exceptional student.

The problem with such favoritism is a failure to see people as God sees them. Solomon reminds us that we are all the creation of God. Wealth, poverty, personal-ity, academic, and athletic skills are by God's design. To favor one over the other is to disregard God's design and providence. When students mock another, they mock his Maker (Prov. 14:31; 17:5). Likewise, 1 Corinthians 8:12 reminds us that when we sin against another Christian we "sin against God."

James reminds us of the other side of the coin (2:1–9)—honoring others for their station in life. When we give preferential treatment to those who are more popular, better looking, or better students, we also mock God. Job declared "For I know not to give flattering titles; in so doing my maker would soon take me away" (Job 32:22).

Final thought: To favor one above another is to mock the wisdom of our Maker!

"A prudent man foreseeth the evil, and hideth himself: but the simple pass on, and are punished."

Wisdom in Foreseeing Future Sin

It is a great part of wisdom to see what God is about to do. When evil comes, most men see it. But the wise *foresee* it.

Two thoughts emerge from this verse: the necessity of foreseeing evil, and the wisdom of fleeing evil. Because students have problems with the first, they often fall prey to the second—"the simple (naïve, immature) pass on, and are punished."

A wise teacher will foresee the adult in the child! She will see the seed of childish temper wrecking a future marriage. She will see the tendency to laziness full-blown in a wasted life. She will see the argumentative spirit leading to an insubordinate employee. She will make the child aware of the future consequences of his childish sins and show him the scriptural steps to correction, thereby enabling him to "hide himself" from the evil.

The simple teacher will pay little attention to such childish sins, so the child will pass on to adulthood and face the evils of his sin. Other teachers will wring their hands, chastise, or punish the child but fail to offer scriptural correction. Thus, they allow the simple to "pass on" to punishment.

Final thought: Children are too simple to see their sin full-grown. We must foresee it for them and give them corrective steps to hide from the evil.

Apple 125

PROVERBS 22:6

"Train up a child in the way he should go: and when he is old, he will not depart from it."

Wisdom in Training

Entire books have been written on this verse as it relates to parents and teachers. The key to the verse lies in understanding the meaning of *train*. The Hebrew means "to initiate, to begin." Its primary use was in the construction of a building. Its secondary use involved the dedication of a building (e.g., the dedication of Solomon's Temple, 1 Kings 8:63; 2 Chron. 7:5). Thus, the word conveys several key ingredients in Christian education. Christian education *initiates* the process of *building* a life that is *dedicated* to the Lord.

The phrase "in the way he should go," is literally "according to his way." *His* most likely refers to *God's* way of wisdom, rather than a man going his own way (Isa. 53:6). This fits with the primary emphasis of Proverbs, which is submission to the Lord and wisdom's way.

Biblical training begins with dedication. Before you begin the process of training your students, you should dedicate each of them individually to the Lord. Nothing is more important for both the child and your attitude toward your class. You are training them to be servants of the Lord, not better citizens. If your mind and motives have been molded by your true mission, you will not be a misguided teacher. Your job is to prepare youth for God's work.

Final thought: Christian educators build living temples for use in God's service. Teach to that end!

Wisdom in Discipling

Training students is far more than teaching. In Jesus' day a teacher was called *master*—a *discipler* of men. The concept is found in Matthew 28:19

"Go ye therefore and *teach* (literally, *disciple*) all nations…." The Great Commission is a call to make disciples, not to simply preach the gospel or to teach facts.

Discipling (teaching) in the Hebrew and Greek culture implied both telling and showing—with the emphasis on *showing*. The master lived with his students. Thus, the master's life, spirit, and attitude were as important as the words he spoke. Today, much of that concept has been lost. The teacher is one who verbally disseminates information but otherwise is not involved in the student's life. As a result, there is little emphasis on commitment, compassion, and creativity in the teaching process. But this is not Christian (New Testament) education.

If we are to be disciplers (masters), then we must learn to teach on three levels: The What, the How, and the Why. The *what* teaches facts, the *how* creatively demonstrates the facts in life situations, and the *why* emphasizes comprehension. If we are not involved in all three steps, we are less than a biblical discipler. Instead, we are only a teacher.

Final thought: Christian educators have a higher calling than just teaching: we are called to disciple!

Apple 127

PROVERBS 22:6

"Train up a child in the way he should go: and when he is old, he will not depart from it."

Wisdom in Teaching More Than Facts

We return to this key verse for yet another look at biblical education. We have seen that a Christian educator is a discipler—training students to be dedicated servants of the Lord. Such training requires three steps: instruction (teaching the *what*); demonstration (teaching the *how*); and comprehension (teaching the *why*).

Do we sell ourselves short by simply teaching the *what*, which is simply disseminating information? The teacher of *what* is a teacher of facts, but he is not a true discipler of youth. While facts and information are necessary for proper biblical education, they are only the first step in the discipling process. Sadly, many educators and educational systems start and stop with this step.

How do we know whether we are a *what* teacher or a true discipler? A *what* teacher emphasizes rote memory. The primary teaching method is lecture and repetition of facts. Tests are designed to measure rote memory skills rather than to demonstrate analytical comprehension of truth. Covering all the material in the curriculum is more important than student comprehension. Thus the *what* teacher rushes along with little time for demonstration or comprehension.

Final thought: What teaching requires little passion, energy, or creativity and produces robots rather than disciples.

PROVERBS 22:6

"Train up a child in the way he should go: and when he is old, he will not depart from it."

Wisdom in Demonstrating Truth

A *master* teacher teaches not only the *what,* but also the *how.* Proverbs 22:6 admonishes us to train children in the *way* they should go (the *how*). Such teaching emphasizes demonstration, both in the laboratory and in life. Which is better—to give students a Rubik's cube and ask them to solve it, or to tell them how without letting them try it? Obviously, the hands-on approach is better. So it is in every aspect of disciple-making. Students may learn facts from your lectures, but they learn their values, morals, priorities, and attitudes from those with whom they interact. Through real life demonstration you will most effectively teach your students.

It is noteworthy that Christ taught while walking, sitting, eating, or riding in a boat. He used current situations, interruptions, and occasions to teach truth. Stones, mustard seeds, barley, fishing nets, fig trees—whatever was at hand—became objects to demonstrate biblical truth. But, most importantly, He taught by the demonstration of His life! Years later John wrote of, "That which we have… seen…and our hands have handled…" (1 John 1:1). This informal interaction with their Master forever transformed the disciples of Christ.

Final thought: The best curriculum is often written by our lives and is taught by interaction with our students in out-of-class situations.

Apple 129

PROVERBS 22:6

"Train up a child in the way he should go: and when he is old, he will not depart from it."

Wisdom in Teaching for Comprehension

Christian education is concerned with comprehension and transformation. The ultimate goal is to see a life forever changed by the power of God ("and when he is old, he will not depart from it"). The discipler knows that he must teach facts, but he recognizes this as only the first step in the discipling (education) process. He creatively demonstrates facts and illustrates how the truth taught is lived in life. His life becomes the model for the student. Ultimately, he wants the truth to take hold of the heart and soul of the student and transform the student's life. He realizes the difference in knowledge and perception (Prov. 1:2). While knowledge is awareness of facts, perception is the ability to explain the reasons behind the facts. But perception is even more than that. Perception occurs when truth grips the heart and changes the life of the student.

A master teacher is one who teaches students to think, not just memorize. In math, instruction requires memorizing math tables. Demonstration illustrates how to use math formulas. Comprehension requires students to think through word problems. In history, instruction requires memorizing dates. Demonstration may use films, pictures, role-playing, or field trips. Comprehension requires them to write essays and/or explain how the historical event affects their lives.

Final thought: Master teachers want truth to master students' lives!

Wisdom in Staying the Course

Ancient cultures recognized the sacredness of the boundary. Even heathen cultures honored the dividing stone as a god not to be touched. Israel's concept of boundaries came from the conviction that God Himself set the bounds of nations, and man must not tamper with them. Thus, "Remove not the ancient landmark (boundary markers), which thy fathers have set."

Christian education also has divinely established boundaries. To move those boundaries is to cease to be truly Christian in our education. Sadly, humanistic approaches to education often pass undetected through the doors of Christian schools. We become curriculum-centered rather than pupil-centered. We aim for the head rather than the heart. We emphasize sports more than spirituality. Academics replaces attitude. Rote memory, rules, and regulations replace righteousness.

Deuteronomy 6:1–9 establishes God's boundaries of education. 1) Disciplers (teachers) must passionately and transparently love the Lord (v. 5). 2) The Word must saturate and grip the teacher's heart (v. 6). 3) Educators must disciple children by modeling truth in every aspect of daily life (v. 7).

Final thought: Don't move the Christian education landmarks: heart over head, consecration over conformity, spirituality over sports, godliness over grades, attitude over academics, children over curriculum, and righteousness over rules!

Apple 131

PROVERBS 23:9

"Speak not in the ears of a fool: for he will despise the wisdom of thy words."

Wisdom in Refraining Words

The Lord's rule is similar. "Give not that which is holy unto the dogs, neither cast ye your pearls before swine…" (Matt. 7:6). Some youth should not be in Christian schools! Obviously, this shouldn't make us trigger happy. So long as there is a grain of hope of reaching a student, we should make every effort for his soul. Like the Master Teacher, we should bring the Word to the worst and the most unwilling, but there is a time to be silent (Eccles. 3:7). Such a time was our Lord's silence before Herod. Herod's heart was not ready for truth.

Christian schools are for Christian youth. Their purpose is to prepare saved youth to love the Lord and the lost passionately, to know His Word and His will, and to submit to His lordship in their lives. Those who openly declare their opposition to God's Word should not be given God's pearls.

Final thought: Aim for the heart before the head. If you can't reach the heart, don't try to reach the head.

P R O V E R B S   2 3 : 1 5

"My son, if thine heart be wise, my heart shall rejoice, even mine."

Wisdom in Aiming for the Heart

What brings you the most joy in teaching? Is it the love of your subject? Is it love for teaching? Is it the delight of seeing students learn? Let's look at what gave Solomon joy.

Solomon focused on his child's heart, not his head. His desire was not that the child might be a great warrior or that he might be successful; his burden was that his child's *heart* might be wise in the things of God. Undoubtedly, he had learned this from his father. In David's old age he challenged Solomon:

"And thou, Solomon, my son, know thou the God of thy father, and serve him with a perfect *heart* and with a willing mind: for the Lord searcheth all *hearts*…if thou seek him, he will be found of thee…" (1 Chron. 28:9).

Christian disciplers must aim for the heart ("if thine *heart* be wise"). An intelligent mind is wasted if the heart is unwise. For God searches the heart of man (1 Sam. 16:7), not the head.

What brings you the most joy in teaching? Is it to see hearts that are tender to the things of God, even if those hearts aren't inside the best students? Is it their hearts that thrill us most or the progress they make in their studies? Obviously, we want both the mind and the heart to be surrendered. But true godliness begins in the heart.

Final thought: The aim of a teacher's heart is to aim for the student's heart.

Apple 133

PROVERBS 23:23

"Buy the truth, and sell it not; also wisdom, and instruction, and understanding."

Wisdom in Appreciating Truth

This passage underscores the value of truth. It is worth buying; it is too valuable to sell! Truth is worth any cost, and nothing can replace its loss.

But what is truth? Pilate ironically asked that question of Jesus who had told His disciples, "I am…the Truth…" (John 14:6). Truth is all that concerns Jesus Christ our Lord. Truth is accepting Him as our personal Lord and Savior and striving to be conformed to His image. All else is but a mirage.

Christian education seeks to change youth's values. It must escalate the value of obedience to God's Word and expose the high cost of disobedience. Even the class valedictorian is not educated if that student is not committed to Christ. Knowledge can be found in books, but true wisdom must come from the Book. A student can succeed academically, but he may, nevertheless, fail to gain truth!

"Sell it not" brings to mind those who sell the Lord for popularity or career advancement. They compromise truth to fulfill their lusts. The teacher must emphasize the value of obedience to God's Word and the cost of disobedience. Many proverbs teach the blessings of wisdom and the folly of disobedience (See the Appendix for numerous verses.) Use these verses in special projects with your students.

Final thought: Proverbs were written to change youthful values. Use them!

Wisdom in Giving Our Heart to God

If you would be a great teacher, give your heart to God! "Oh, but I gave my heart to the Lord when I was saved," you may say. Salvation is only the first step in giving our heart to Him. Solomon has a further step in mind in this passage. You must empty your heart of all that keeps your mind off Him, and then fill your heart with thoughts of His glory.

Deuteronomy 6:4–6 reflects this idea:

"These words that I command thee this day, shall be in *thine heart,* and thou shalt teach them…." Though these passages were addressed to parents, the principle applies to all who teach children: A God–filled heart precedes effective teaching.

How do we fill our hearts with God? We fill our hearts with Him by filling our *eyes* with His ways ("and let thine eyes observe my ways"). We do this by reading His Word with an eye toward noting how God operates. *Observing* in the Hebrew means *pleasure, delight,* or *pleasing.* We are to delight in His ways. We must take pleasure in noticing how God operates in given situations. A wise teacher will fill his eyes with God's ways and keep a "How God Works" notebook to record his observations. His God–filled eyes will result in a God–filled heart. Nothing is more vital. Give your heart over to God by filling your mind with Him!

Final thought: A God–filled heart precedes a God–filled class.

Apple 135

PROVERBS 24:13-14

"My son, eat thou honey, because it is good; and the honeycomb, which is sweet to thy taste: So shall the knowledge of wisdom be unto thy soul: when thou hast found it, then there shall be a reward, and thy expectation shall not be cut off."

Wisdom in Feeding Our Minds

Nothing is sweeter than honey. We eat it with delight. Such is the sweetness of God's Word. Like the honeycomb, it is delightful and energizing to the godly. David calls God's Word sweeter than the honeycomb (Ps. 19:10) and again "sweeter than honey to my mouth" (Ps. 119:103).

But the sweetness of God's Word is an acquired taste! Hebrews 5:14 reminds us that the enjoyment of God's Word belongs to those "that are of full age, even those who by reason of use have their senses exercised to discern both good and evil." In other words, God's Word is not as tasty to some as to others. What makes it sweeter to some? The continual use and exercise of the Word makes it sweeter. Daily, habitual meditation on God in the Word improves with use! At first the believer finds it difficult to understand and enjoy (Ps. 119:25–28). But eventually he can say, "How sweet are thy words to my taste" (Ps. 119:104).

Final thought: A teacher is not mentally fit until his soul delights in the sweetness of God's Word.

PROVERBS 24:13-14

"My son, eat thou honey, because it is good; and the honeycomb, which is sweet to thy taste: So shall the knowledge of wisdom be unto thy soul: when thou hast found it, then there shall be a reward, and thy expectation shall not be cut off."

Wisdom in Discovering God's Word

What is the sweetness of *wisdom* described in this passage? I suggest two things: 1) the sweetness of God's Person that permeates His Word; and 2) the sweetness of discovery!

As to the sweetness of God's Person, we must realize that His Word was given to reveal Him! If we only see facts, stories, and information in His Word, we see little more than the unsaved. Believers, however, should see God's glorious character in every verse and passage. The wise reader will learn to focus on God in the Word, rather than focus on the Word of God!

As to the sweetness of discovery, we will be blessed "when thou hast found it." What is *it* that is found? Is it not when our eyes discover a truth we had not seen before? Is it not when what once looked like a single grain of truth opens to become a field of waving barley? Is it not when we begin to see glimpses of His glory in every passage we read? Ah, this is true sweetness! As the gold miner cries "Eureka" when he strikes a vein of gold, so we cry "Hallelujah" when our once dull eyes glimpse His glory in the Word!

Final thought: If you struggle in the Word, keep digging. By reason of use you will soon discover the sweetness of His Word!

Apple 137

PROVERBS 24:16

"For a just man falleth seven times, and riseth up again: but the wicked shall fall into mischief."

Wisdom in Handling the Easily Discouraged

Not all rebels are rebels! As we have noted previously, 1 Thessalonians 5:14 describes three types of problem youth: the rebel, the easily discouraged, and the weak (or the unruly, feebleminded, and weak). All may appear to be rebellious, but that's only an outward facade. The easily discouraged may slump in his seat, mumble when he talks, pay little attention in class, or fail to do his work. However, his heart—unlike the rebellious—wants to do right, but he thinks he can't! The easily discouraged give up easily. Some are perfectionists and would rather do nothing than try and fail. Others are insecure and lack the confidence to try. Either way they are defeated by defeat. If they once fail, they quit. They need encouragement, not criticism.

Have them memorize this verse. Show them that even the greatest athletes fall on the court, but they don't lie there. They get up and try again. Challenge them to get up, to claim this verse, and to go out and try it again! Only the wicked fall into mischief. This is a different Hebrew word from *falleth*. This word means to fall due to a physical condition (i.e., a rebellious heart). They don't get up because they are spiritually dead.

Final thought: Both the just and the wicked fall. The difference is found in who gets up!

PROVERBS 24:27

"Prepare thy work without, and make it fit for thyself in the field; and afterwards build thine house."

Wisdom in Preparation

Youth often want the house without the work! They want good grades without studying. They want to succeed without discipline and sweat. This verse reminds us that before the house comes the work. There must be *preparation in the street* ("prepare thy work without") and *making ready the field* before one can build the house. Nice homes and cars are the result of long years of diligent work. The things adults enjoy are due to sacrifice and sweat, not the lottery! This is a difficult lesson for youth who live in a get–rich–quick society.

Teachers must learn this lesson as well. If youth are *houses,* we build them through careful preparation. Godly students are the result of prayer, filling our heart with the Word, deepening our relationship with the Lord, and using the Word to counsel our students. Christian schools don't automatically produce godly graduates. They are the result of diligent heart preparation by dedicated teachers with one goal—the godliness of the student. Sadly, some spend more time in lesson preparation than in heart preparation because they are more focused on students' grades than their godliness.

Final thought: Before we build godly youth, we prepare the field of our heart.

Apple 139

PROVERBS 24:33-34

"Yet a little sleep, a little slumber, a little folding of the hands to sleep: So shall thy poverty come as one that travelleth; and thy want as an armed man."

Wisdom in Redeeming the Time

Charles Spurgeon is our teacher today.

T*he worst of sluggards only ask for a little slumber; they would be indignant if they were accused of thorough idleness…Yet by littles the day ebbs out, and the time for labour is all gone, and the field is grown over with thorns. It is by little procrastinations that men ruin their souls. They have no intention to delay for years—a few months will bring the more convenient season—tomorrow if you will, they will attend to serious things; but the present hour is so occupied and altogether so unsuitable, that they beg to be excused. Like sands from an hourglass, time passes, life is wasted by driblets, and seasons of grace lost by little slumbers. Oh, to be wise, to catch the flying hour, to use the moments on the wing."*

Such were men's thoughts at the close of the 19th century. If so then, more so now! A century has brought us more ease and entertainment to distract us from the urgency of the hour. Yet are we not nearer the final days than then? Satan would steal the hearts of our youth. It is "high time to awake out of sleep: for now is our salvation nearer than when we believed" (Rom. 13:11). The enemy of idleness is at the door to steal the hearts of our youth.

Final thought: Carpe diem—seize the day lest the enemy seize our youth!

"It is the glory of God to conceal a thing: but the honour of kings is to search out a matter."

Wisdom in Searching God's Glory

God's glory is unfathomable. What glory could belong to a God whose name, ways, and works could be fully understood by mortal man? We look at His ways and discover that "thy way is in the sea, and thy path in the great waters, and thy footsteps are not known" (Ps. 77:19). We view His forgiveness and realize that no human wisdom can understand the full extent of His grace. We view His work in creation and salvation and proclaim, "O the depth of the riches both of the wisdom and knowledge of God! How unsearchable *are* his judgments, and his ways past finding out" (Rom. 11:33). Charles Bridges asked, "Are not the clouds of His concealment the brightness of His glory?"

By contrast, the glory of kings is to search out knowledge! We know nothing compared to the vast universe of God's knowledge. It is our glory to spend our days searching out the *unsearchable riches of Christ* (Eph. 3:8). But though we spend our lifetime in searching out His glory in all we see, we would catch but a glimpse of the edge of His brightness. For who could see His full brightness (Exo. 33:20) who "dwelleth in the light which no man can approach unto" (1 Tim. 6:16)?

Final thought: The glory of your teaching is to reveal His glory in every subject you teach. He is there. Search Him out and reveal Him to your class!

Apple 141

PROVERBS 25:2

"It is the glory of God to conceal a thing: but the honour of kings is to search out a matter."

Wisdom in a Leaf, Part 1

Some things are too small to be seen; others are too large. Can we with the naked eye see the tiny atom or the far reaches of the universe? One is too minute to be seen and the other is too vast—yet in both the glory of God is concealed. It is man's glory to search out the King's glory in all of His creation. The next three days we will search out His glory in a leaf! Read the following and record on the following page what you see of God's glory from the tiny leaf.

We could not live without leaves! They are amazing solar factories that manufacture food for plants. Without this food, plants could not live. Without plants, animals and humans could not live. Leaves provide man with shade, oxygen, and moisture (an elm transpires one ton of water a day into our atmosphere), and they beautify the earth. The largest leaf is the South American palm, measuring 26' x 5'. The smallest is the wolfie, which gives ponds their greenish tint. The most numerous leaf is the diatom, which is invisible without a microscope. They are found in every drop of water on the surface of oceans, and they provide 90% of the food for fish. Each is a beautiful work of art with hard transparent crystal covers marked with beautiful variegated colors. There are billions of oak leaves, but no two are identical!

Final thought: If God's glory is concealed in a leaf, what must be in the sun!

Apple 142

PROVERBS 25:2

"It is the glory of God to conceal a thing: but the honour of kings is to search out a matter."

Wisdom in a Leaf, Part 2

God's glory is inexhaustible. It is in all we see, yet we don't see it! The angels declared:

"Holy, holy, holy, *is* the LORD of hosts: the whole earth *is* full of his glory." The universe is but a giant theater to reveal the concealed glory of God. It is our glory (i.e., the greatest thing we can do), to search it out and share it with others. Let's continue searching out His glory in a tiny leaf. Read the following and continue to record the things you see of His glory on the page provided.

Each leaf is like a room. It has a floor and a roof supported by thousands of tiny pillars. Inside this room food is manufactured. Sunlight filters through the transparent roof above. The floor below has up to 100,000 stomata (mouths) per inch, that open and close to let in air. Two "guards" stand at each stomata to see that the right amount of oxygen and water enter the room.

The pillars (palisades) are covered with green chemical specks which we call chlorophyll. The filtered sun strikes the chlorophyll, initiating a chemical reaction called photosynthesis. When carbon and other elements of the air entering through the stomata change to starch, sugar, and oil, the result is food!

It takes 12 banana leaves to produce 60 pounds of bananas, fifteen leaves to produce a cluster of grapes, thirty leaves to produce a peach, and fifty leaves to make an apple!

Final thought: Good teachers are glory–miners, digging out God's glory in every subject they teach! What riches have you mined today?

Apple 143

PROVERBS 25:2

"It is the glory of God to conceal a thing: but the honour of kings is to search out a matter."

Wisdom in a Leaf, Part 3

It has been our glory to search out His glory in a tiny leaf. Compare your notes from the past two days with what follows. Perhaps you saw some things that we will not mention. Such is the depth of His glory. Though we plumb the depths or scale the heights for a thousand years, we could see but the corona of His glory! Notice God's glory in the leaf:

- His infinite wisdom—Who of us could have thought of such a thing when it did not exist?

- His perfect order and design—God created the amazing symmetry and efficiency of a solar unit by placing the smallest solar factory known to man inside the leaf.

- His infinite knowledge—He knows everything about solar power, even things we are only now discovering.

- His care and provision for man—He provides us with shade, beauty, and food through a leaf, displaying His concern for us.

- His infinite detail—His attention to minute details of design are seen in the stomata, the palisades, the transparent roof, and the little guards that regulate the intake of oxygen and water.

- His omnipotence—God's power is seen in the power to make such a machine and in the power of that machine to make food.

- His efficiency—In the leaf, nothing is wasted. Even dying leaves provide beauty, enrich the soil, and provide much needed exercise for man in raking them.

Final thought: Psalm 104:24, "O Lord, how manifest are thy works! In wisdom hast thou made them all: the earth is full of thy riches." Here is how we teach science, history, geography, math, and language. His glory is in them all!

"Take away the dross from the silver, and there shall come forth a vessel for the finer. Take away the wicked from before the king, and his throne shall be established in righteousness."

Wisdom in Seeing Beyond the Slag

The principle is simple: the refining process produces silver for the smith. The applications are many:

1. Organizations (national, church, school, business) must purge the wicked from their midst before the Lord will bless (the application Solomon uses here).

2. Believers must be cleansed of sin to be fit for the Master's use (2 Tim. 2:21).

3. The fires of persecution and trial produce patience, character, and beauty of soul.

4. The refiner (teacher/parent) sees beauty in the dirty slag and refines it for the silversmith (the Lord) to work his craft and produce a vessel of beauty and value.

All of these apply to a school. As stated in an earlier devotional, not all students should be in a Christian school. There are times when students and leaders must both be purged from a school to preserve the integrity and spirit of the institution.

The wise teacher sees pure silver in the most insubordinate and least promising child in her class and works to remove the dross, so that God may produce the vessel. Teacher, look beyond the mischievous and immature student and see the shining silver beyond the dross.

Final thought: Beyond the dross is silver God can use. Your worst student may be tomorrow's godly leader! Don't give up! Refine, refine, refine.

Apple 145

PROVERBS 25:11

"A word fitly spoken is like apples of gold in pictures of silver."

Wisdom in Gracious Speech

Apples of gold resting in baskets of silver filigree—such is the picture Solomon uses of proper speech. The allusion teaches us much about the speech of the wise.

First, our speech must be "fitly spoken." That is, it must be appropriate for the moment—words that fit the occasion. Job declares, "How forcible are right words" (Job 6:25). Our Lord Himself was concerned with right words for the right moment, saying that the Father hath "given me the tongue of the learned, that I should know how to speak a word in season to him that is weary" (Isa. 50:4). Rotten apples in silver filigree baskets are a disgrace. Choose your words well. They must be used in good taste—with decorum, control, and grace.

Fitly spoken is literally "words upon the wheels," that is, words that flow naturally, unforced, rolling smoothly from the occasion. Christ's discourses on the living water and the bread of life arose naturally out of conversation, making them much more powerful.

Words upon the wheels also implies planned speech. Most unsavory fruit is placed in the basket when we speak by impulse and irritation.

Further, speaking upon the wheels indicates repetition. Solomon repeats similar Proverbs to the slothful, the scorner, and the fool. As wagon wheels running over the same ground create a path, so thoughts revisited stick in the mind.

Final thought: Golden apples grow on cultivated trees. Fill your mind with His Word if you would fill your mouth with His words.

"He that hath no rule over his own spirit is like a city that is broken down, and without walls."

Wisdom in Self–Control

The easiest way for Satan to enter a school is through the loss of self-control! Every fit of uncontrolled anger breaches the walls of our spirit and allows the enemy to gain entrance. Once he breaches the walls, the angry soul fires unfit words, like hot arrows in every direction, "as a madman who casteth firebrands, arrows, and death" (Prov. 26:18). The careless get hit or hurt. His words cut deep, and even the innocent are wounded. Thus, the teacher who cannot control his spirit wounds his class. How opposite the scene of those words are apples of gold in pictures of silver!

How do we maintain our defenses against injurious, angry speech? Charles Bridges speaks of one defense:

"Every outbreaking of irritation, every spark of pride kindling in the heart, must be attacked, and determinately resisted. It is the beginning of a breach in the walls of the city. Without instant attention, it will widen to the ruin of the whole…. Effective self–control is divine grace, not one's own native power. What then is to be done? On the first assault fortify the walls by prayer. Trust not in the strength of the citadel."

We may add another line of defense: filling our minds with the Word of God. "Thy word have I hid in mine heart, that I might not sin against thee" (Ps. 119:11). Fortify your mind with verses that deal with the sin of anger and intemperance. God's Word acts as a secondary wall to keep anger from bursting forth in a volcanic explosion of fire and violence.

Final thought: Fits of uncontrolled temper make one unfit to teach!

Apple 147

PROVERBS 26:1

"As snow in summer, and as rain in harvest, so honor is not seemly for a fool."

Wisdom in Giving Honor

Paul beseeches us to give honor to whom honor is due (Rom. 13:7). Solomon reveals him to whom honor is not due—the fool. There are two main Hebrew words for *fool* in Proverbs—*kesil*, and *ewil*. The former comes from a word meaning to be *sluggish, fat, dull*. I call him the Pig-headed Fool. He doesn't care what people say or think. He is often lazy, sloppy, and uncaring. The latter term describes someone who is hot-headed and stubborn. I call him the Bull-headed Fool. He rushes in with impulse, temper, and lack of self-control.

In this case, the Pig-headed Fool is not to be honored. Here is one who doesn't listen to advice or instruction. You can show him how, but it's as though he was never instructed. Stubbornly and dully he plods along, refusing to listen or to care. To honor him is as unfitting as snow in the middle of summer or as a heavy rain that drowns the field at the time of harvest.

The principle is applicable in a Christian school. We often make the mistake of honoring the athlete, or the cool crowd—even though they may be ungodly in their life—by choosing them as captain, calling on them to pray, naming them the MVP, giving them the lead role in a play, or giving them the solo part in a musical. Sadly, the student body knows what they do on weekends, or in the locker-room, or when adults aren't around. Such honor brings disgrace to godliness and discourages those who truly love the Lord.

Final thought: We dishonor God when we honor the godless.

Wisdom in Dealing with Excuses

Teachers know excuses! They have heard them all. I once told a teacher I was late to class because I had a problem with my eyes. That was true. I couldn't get them open in the morning due to a malady called sleep. The truth is that most excuses are a cover for laziness. The slothful student claims he couldn't do his homework because there was a lion in the street.

How must we treat excuses? First, realize that every child is a sinner, and deceit is born in his heart. The wise teacher is not gullible to excuses. But neither should the teacher suspect every excuse. Legitimate reasons sometimes interfere with duties, and teachers must be as sensitive to these as they are suspicious of others. Nothing is worse than doubting truth! It sends a signal to the student that you question his character.

Second, see slothfulness behind most lame excuses, and be ready to deal with it biblically. Use verses such as this when students make up excuses for their failure. Show them their real problem—laziness. Call it what God calls it—the sin of slothfulness.

Third, help them overcome their slothfulness. Tell them you want to help them overcome this debilitating sin. Ask them to search Proverbs for every occurrence of the word *slothful* (11 occasions) to write out each verse and what it means. Use these verses each time they show a slothful tendency.

Finally, be sure to compliment them for the progress they make. Commend them in front of the class. Don't leave them with the impression they are a hopeless sloth!

Final thought: There is no excuse for laziness.

Apple 149

PROVERBS 26:16

"The sluggard is wiser in his own conceit than seven men that can render a reason."

Wisdom in Overcoming Sluggishness

Once more we meet the lazy man! This is the last of a four–verse stanza on the slothful. As we study Proverbs we see this man often. Evidently, it is a characteristic God despises in a believer. Two Hebrew words are used repeatedly to describe this man. One word means to be slow, idle, and lazy. It describes one who refuses to work (Prov. 6:6); who loves excessive sleep (6:9); who makes up excuses for not working (26:13); who is too lazy to eat (19:24; 26:15); who irritates those for whom he works (10:26); and whose fields (i.e., room, house, locker, desk) are unkempt or overgrown with weeds and thorns (24:30–34).

The other word means to be slack or negligent. It describes those who do not take pride in their work but aim to get by with the least amount of effort.

The problem with both is described here as conceit. He will argue with seven men, wiser than he, and not change his ways. He considers himself a genius and prides himself in how efficiently he avoids work! He has found ways to avoid exertion and doesn't realize that he is lazy.

Until now we have applied these verses to our students. Let's apply them now to teachers! In what respect are we influenced by the conceit of slothfulness? Does it affect our lesson preparation, our energy in the class, or giving ourselves to counsel? Does it affect the time we spend on our knees or in Bible reading? Do we let little aches and pains keep us from our work while convincing ourselves that it really hurts worse than it does?

Final thought: Heaven will never be won by folded arms! "The violent take it by force" (Matt. 11:12).

PROVERBS 26:18–19

"As a mad man who casteth firebrands, arrows, and death, So is the man that deceiveth his neighbor, and saith, Am not I in sport?"

Wisdom in Sobriety

Youth are often violent. Cruelty flows from their mouth as easily as water over a dam. Little do they realize that the barbs and taunts they throw at those less gifted may be as violent as shooting them with a gun. They are totally unaware of the misery they bring upon others. They bear no malice, but they simply don't think. Their buddies laugh with them and join in triumph over the victim. But God describes them as a "mad man" scattering "firebrands, arrows, and death."

When fun is in good taste, it is harmless. However, when practical jokes (innocent as they may seem), mockery, or teasing deceives or wounds its victim, or goes beyond the bounds of godliness, it ceases to be *sport*. It then becomes violence on the playground!

Teachers must be sensitive to this malady among youth. They must not allow a student to be the butt of cruel jokes. Neither must they allow the class to laugh at others' failures, physical attributes, or appearance.

Teachers must also avoid laughing at their students or belittling them in front of others. Mocking students, playing practical jokes on them, or laughing at their failure is devastating to both the teacher and the class. It is as destructive to the teacher's effectiveness as it is demoralizing to the student. The wise teacher is thoughtful of her students' feelings and outlaws violent words. Matthew Henry warns, "He that sins in jest, must repent in earnest; or his sin will be his ruin."

Final thought: Words can kill.

Apple 151

PROVERBS 27:5

"Open rebuke is better than secret love."

Wisdom in Expressing Love

Not everyone knows how to express their love. Childhood abuse, lack of outward expressions of love from parents, embarrassment, spurned love, or deep insecurity all may contribute to the concealment of affection. Though they love, they have difficulty expressing it. Yet God says it is better to rebuke someone openly than to love them but never show it.

A teacher must overcome such tendencies. He must be open, transparent, and loving of his students. Did Jesus not openly express His love for us in coming to earth to die for our sins? We may be afraid to express our love for fear of being rejected, but Christ expressed His love though He *knew* He would be spurned. Such is the kind of love a teacher needs for her class.

How do we express our love for our students? We love them first by telling them that we love them. You may be the only person they hear say those three magic words. We also love them by giving our time and attention to them when they speak. We look them in the eye and listen carefully to what they say. We express our love by doing little things for them. You may never know the impact your simple gesture may have.

But we also show our love by rebuking them when they fail. A true friend will not let those he loves fall into hurtful sin or harmful habits. He will love them enough to confront them with Scripture. "Open rebuke is better than secret love."

Final thought: Expressions of love are more important than claims of love. Give them your attention, your time, your thoughtfulness, your counsel, and, when needed, your loving rebuke.

"The full soul loatheth an honeycomb; but to the hungry soul every bitter thing is sweet."

Wisdom in Discerning the Hungry Soul

Not every child hungers for spiritual growth! This is true in the natural realm. Abundance, instead of increasing happiness, deprives one of joy! Boredom sets in and apathy follows. Yet the poor, hungry for the goods of the rich, strive to have what the rich man loathes. Israel, filled with "angel's food," loathed and trod it under foot as "light bread."

Is this not also true in the realm of the spiritual? The Laodicean church "rich and increased with goods" loathed the honeycomb of the Word (Rev. 3:17–18). So are those who have not been born again. They may read the Bible but only because they have to or to find some curious fact. They may even seek to belittle its most precious truths.

Note the hungry souls in your class, and feed them the Bread of Life. You will see them during Bible class or devotions. They will be like boys at a picnic: first in line, with fork and plate in hand! There they sit, with Bibles open, pen in hand, taking notes, and asking questions. When the class has devotions, they don't twiddle their thumbs. They meditate, and voluntarily pray, and keep a prayer list, and sometimes weep for their friends.

Teacher, how's your spiritual appetite? Do you long for His Word? Do you have an insatiable hunger to grow? Are even the hard truths of the Word, which convict of sin, sweet to your soul? Do you hungrily glean, even when the preacher gives but the most meager of food? "Blessed are they that hunger and thirst after righteousness, for they shall be filled."

Final thought: Only a hungry teacher can produce a hungry class!

Apple 153

PROVERBS 27:8

"As a bird that wandereth from her nest, so is a man that wandereth from his place."

Wisdom in Knowing Yourself

As the bird is safest in her nest, so is man safest where he belongs. The problem is that many of us don't know where we belong in life.

The *discontented* wander from one job to another. No place is large enough for their talents. Thus, like the bird who has lost his nest, they flit from one place to another, seeking their dream, but finding none.

The *gifted* is full of zeal for God. His gifts should not be wasted in such a small school, or on such a tiny class. Should he not be the administrator? Could he not do a better job? But is he not wandering from his place? The Lord's command is, "Give an account of *thy* (not another's) stewardship" (Luke 16:2). Our wisdom is to understand *our own way* (Prov. 16:8), and to do *our own business* (1 Thess. 4:11).

The *unsteady* finds no church sound enough for him. He wanders from church to church until he discovers another inconsistency, and he is away again.

The *dreamer* cannot find his dream. Perhaps he will be this. Perhaps not—he would rather be that. He will be a doctor of philosophy, though he stays not in school but for a year. Then he is off to chase another dream.

The *wise* know what they can do and what they cannot do. The wise know that God requires but one thing—faithfulness where He has planted them. "Brethren, let every man, wherein he is called, therein abide with God" (1 Cor. 7:24).

Final thought: Stick to the nest until God moves you.

Wisdom in Personalizing Our Teaching, Part 1

M an is made for companionship" (Bridges). Without social interaction we would be miserable. We would lose the ability to communicate. We would lose our motivation for living and our creativity. The collision of minds whets the edges of both, as steel sharpens the edge of a knife.

Some of the most valuable discoveries of science are due to teamwork. One has an idea, another has an improvement, and a third adds the final component. There are many examples in the Bible. David had Jonathan, Naomi had Ruth, and Timothy had Paul. Paul was often refreshed by the countenance of his friends (Acts 18:5; 28:14; 2 Cor. 7:6). The Lord sent the disciples out in pairs. The Church was formed on this basis. Thus, we are not to forsake the assembling of ourselves together (Heb. 10:24–25).

Likewise, students need a teacher. But they need more than an instructor in class. They need the camaraderie of the teacher in informal situations! Our Lord did not teach in a classroom but in the milieu of life. You may accomplish more with your students on the playground or in the lunchroom than in the classroom.

Final thought: Your students need you as much as they need your teaching!

Apple 155

PROVERBS 27:19

"As in water face answereth to face, so the heart of man to man."

Wisdom in Personalizing Our Teaching, Part 2

When one looks in water (or in a mirror), he sees a reflection of his own face. Thus, *face answereth to face*. Herein is a lesson for educators: Head speaks to head. What we know in our head, we teach to our students' heads. Information is passed from our head to the head of our students. This is informational teaching (as we have learned in a previous devotional).

The Christian classroom, however, is interested in heart instruction, and only a heart can teach another heart: "…so the heart of man to man."

If heads teach through words, how do hearts teach? Hearts teach through interpersonal relationships, and hearts learn by observation. Thus, our hearts reach the hearts of our students when we mingle with them outside the classroom. As heads teach facts, so hearts teach values. Someone has said, "Values are caught rather than taught." Heads cannot teach values because that is the job of the heart. As students observe the values we live outside the classroom, their hearts are affected. As they see our excitement about the Lord, they get excited.

Thus, it behooves us to make sure our hearts are on fire for God and that we spend time with our students so that their hearts can catch that fire!

Final thought: Be a heart teacher, not just a head teacher.

PROVERBS 27:18

"Whoso keepeth the fig tree shall eat the fruit thereof: so he that waiteth on his master shall be honored."

Wisdom in Serving

Teachers get discouraged. The pay is not great. Often they are under-appreciated. Students and parents complain. The hours are long. They need this verse!

The fig tree was a valuable product in Judea (Mic. 4:4; Hab. 3:17; Luke 13:6) that provided nourishment and sustenance in a non-refrigerated world! Yet those who tended the fig were considered lower-class citizens in the eyes of most. Nevertheless, the keeper of the fig tree was recompensed by eating its fruit.

Likewise, those who faithfully serve their master will be rewarded. Elisha's devotion to Elijah was honored with a double portion of his spirit (2 Kings 2:3-5). So, too, is the Christian teacher who faithfully discharges her duties rewarded. Our happiness is in our students. Paul's converts were his hope, joy, and crown (Phil. 4:1; 1 Thess. 2:19).

Further, the Master has promised "...if any man serve me, him will my Father honor" (John 12:26). A day is coming when the Son of Glory will Himself present us before the assembled world, "Well-done, thou good and faithful servant: thou hast been faithful over a few things, I will make thee ruler over many things: enter thou into the joy of thy Lord" (Matt. 25:21).

Final thought: Our greatest reward is yet ahead—when we shall see His face and His name shall be on our foreheads (Rev. 22:3-4)!

Apple 157

PROVERBS 27:23
"Be thou diligent to know the state of thy flocks, and look well to thy herds."

Wisdom in Knowing Our Students

Teachers, like pastors, are shepherds. Their students are their flock. And, like shepherds, they must be diligent to know the state of each of their sheep. In ancient times, every sheep was precious. It was a grief to lose one to the lion or the bear. So David "fed them according to the integrity of his heart: and guided them by the skillfulness of his hands" (Ps. 78:72). Whether the object of his integrity was the sheep that he led as a youth, or the people that he led as an adult, he led them with the same integrity and care.

It is imperative that we, likewise, shepherd our students. We must be *diligent to know the state* of each child in our class. We look beyond their appearance, their behavior, or their personality. We consider their home—whether their parents are lost or saved, godly or ungodly, caring or uncaring. We consider whether they have physical, mental, or spiritual problems. We discover their strengths and weaknesses and learn how best to reach each one. One needs praise; another needs kindness; yet another needs a touch or rebuke. No two are the same. Each must be treated differently. Do you as diligently study your students as you study your curriculum and lesson plans? It is not curriculum we teach, but students!

Final thought: Knowing your students is as important as knowing your subject.

Wisdom in Discerning Guilt

Teachers must discern sin behind behavior. Often what appears to be fear, or lack of confidence, or the inability to concentrate, may be the result of a deeper problem—unconfessed sin. If you deal only with the fruit and fail to discover the root, you will not help the student.

What are the signs of guilt?

- Guilt causes youth to hide from God and God's people (Gen. 3:8; Isa. 2:19; Luke 5:8).
- Guilty youth are uncomfortable around godly people. They do not enjoy prayer, devotional times, or chapel. They appear to be secretive and devious.
- Guilt diverts the eyes from looking up (Ezek. 9:6). Ezra's guilt kept him from looking up at God, and guilty youth often divert their eyes from looking at an authority figure. They would rather look down than up.

- Guilt produces restlessness (Ps. 38:3).
- Guilt often produces uneasiness, anger, and a quick temper in a child.
- Guilt robs joy and happiness (Ps. 32:3; 38:4).
- Guilt–ridden youth are sullen, they don't sing, and they would rather smirk than laugh.
- Guilt may produce physical problems (Ps. 32:3–4).
- Guilt causes lack of concentration (Ps. 51:3). Preoccupation with guilt robs a child of the ability to concentrate in class.
- Guilt separates youth from God (Isa. 59:2).

Final thought: Dealing with the fruit but not the root is like putting a band–aid on cancer!

Apple 159

PROVERBS 28:1

"The wicked flee when no man pursueth; but the righteous are bold as a lion."

Wisdom in Detecting Innocence

The signs of a righteous person will also help us to detect a guilty person because their characteristics are completely opposite.

- Righteous youth have nothing to hide, so they are open and transparent. They often "spill their guts" (like a first grader who tells all to the consternation of his parents).

- Righteous youth enjoy prayer time, chapel, and devotions. They ask questions, and they get involved (Ps. 140:13).

- Righteous youth are at peace with themselves and everyone else. They have anger under control and enjoy life (Ps. 55:22; 72:7).

- Righteous youth are happy and laugh easily. They sing without shame, and are enthusiastic and energetic in activities (Ps. 32:11; 64:10).

- Righteous youth have a better ability to concentrate because their mind is clear of guilt.

The purpose of the past two devotionals is to aid the teacher in dealing with the root of a child's problems rather than the fruit. If we concentrate on their misbehavior in chapel, their sullen spirit, their temper, or their dislike for looking us in the eye, we will never correct the problem! Somewhere within there is a sin that must be cleansed. It may be a sin of which the child is unaware—a failure to forgive someone for an offense, or bitterness toward an abusive parent. Or it may be a sin weighing heavily on the mind. Either way, it must be rooted out.

Final thought: Behind the fruit lies the root. Dig for it with probing questions.

Wisdom in Education

True education is God–focused. Only one who knows the Lord is capable of teaching truth, and if truth is not taught, education has not taken place. But knowing God in salvation is not the same as seeking the Lord. "They that seek the Lord understand all things." This phrase is paramount in Israel's history. The Chronicles record the phrase 28 times. Every king that was blessed prepared his heart to seek the Lord. Every king that was wicked did not prepare his heart to seek the Lord.

What does it mean to seek the Lord in education? It is the effort to see God in every discipline you teach—whether math, the sciences, grammar, literature, sociology, history, geography, or health.

A few weeks ago we saw God in a leaf. He is also in the sun, in the perfect order of mathematics, and in the laws of grammar. History is His story. Geography is by His design. He is the plumb line by which all literature must be judged.

To teach youth about God only when we teach Bible is to fail. There is no history or science without Him. Only if you seek to portray His character and majesty in every discipline you teach, do you truly understand what you teach! Just as the Pharisees searched the Scriptures (John 5:39) but failed to see Jesus, so we may study our subject well yet fail to see the Lord in it.

Final thought: If you fail to display God in every subject you teach, you fail to teach.

Apple 161

PROVERBS 28:13

"He that covereth his sins shall not prosper: but whoso confesseth and forsaketh them shall have mercy."

Wisdom in Honesty

Honesty is of paramount importance in reaching youth. Youth are brutally honest—ranging from vulgarity to spilling their guts. They hate pretense. The 1960's revolution was to some extent a rebellion against what they saw as gross hypocrisy in the American political and economic systems. Yet youth are sometimes the greatest pretenders in society. They cover up sin with politeness and feigned innocence. They have two standards: what they expect from adults and what they do when they're in trouble.

Of course, God has a standard too. His standard is holiness or righteousness. Both terms imply the absence of impurity (including all forms of deception) and the presence of righteous behavior. God will give mercy to those who honestly admit and forsake their sins.

We please both God and man when we are honest. We sometimes use arguments against various sins that don't hold water. When youth challenge those fallacious arguments, don't be a hard head! Admit the fallacy. That doesn't mean the sin is right; it just means one of your arguments wasn't credible. By admitting it, you gain the students' confidence. By refusing to be honest, you lose your credibility.

Final thought: Youth will listen better to the teacher who admits, "I don't know," or "I was wrong" than to the teacher who is always right!

"He that rebuketh a man afterwards shall find more favour than he that flattereth with the tongue."

Wisdom in Godly Rebuke

R ebuke is rarely easy for the giver or the receiver. However, *afterwards* (some-times long afterwards) the rebuked learns to appreciate the friend who had the courage to rebuke him and save him from a world of harm.

"Flattery will not help a student. Solomon portrays flattery as lying with evil intent (Prov. 26:28), but it can also be simply telling someone what they want to hear…" (The Complete Biblical Library). Either way, it does more harm than good.

The Hebrew word for *rebuke* means to convict in the legal sense. It is to show the offender, through powerful scriptural arguments, that he is wrong and that his sin will cost him dearly. It is not the same as *fussing,* nor is it the same as venting your anger on a child's misdeeds. It is not ranting and raving.

Biblical rebuke is counseling. It is calmly and kindly using the Bible to show a child that he is a sinner, the true name of his sin (lying, stealing, dishonesty, greed, judging others, gossip, adultery, drunkenness), and the penalty for his sin. When it is executed with Scripture, it convinces the youth of his sin, humbles him before God, and leads him to confession. Biblical rebuke should be followed by *instruction in righteousness* (2 Tim. 3:16), which involves sharing biblical steps to overcome the sin.

Final thought: Do you rant and rave, or do you rebuke? Only the latter, done with the Bible in hand, will prosper your students.

Apple 163

PROVERBS 28:26

"He that trusteth in his own heart is a fool: but whoso walketh wisely, he shall be delivered."

Wisdom in Self–Distrust

The flesh trusts nothing but itself! We have a natural distrust of everything but self. Some can't relax when others drive the car. Some can't designate responsibility because no one else could do it right. Over time we learn to trust our own judgment, wisdom, experience, and decision–making. This is seen in how little we pray or how seldom we seek the advice of others.

Yet is our heart not an imposter? The Bible says it is desperately wicked. "To trust an imposter, who has deceived us a hundred times, or a traitor, who has proved himself false to our best interests, is surely to deserve the name of *fool*" (Charles Bridges).

Israel defeated Jericho with fear and trembling and by seeking God's face. Next they faced Ai. But there was no fear, trembling, or prayer! They knew what to do. They had beaten a much stronger enemy at Jericho. They trusted their experience and their superior numbers and were shamefully defeated.

The more experience we have, the less we pray. We have learned the *best* way. We have been down this road before. We have our lesson plans well-polished. We have taught the same curriculum for years. We know how to handle children, so we don't pray.

Final thought: How little we pray is a measure of how big a fool we are! We are wisest when we walk on our knees.

"When the righteous are in authority, the people rejoice: but when the wicked beareth rule, the people mourn."

Wisdom in Righteousness

Are you a righteous teacher? A righteous teacher is a believer. He has trusted Christ as His Lord and Savior and has had the righteousness of Christ imputed (charged) to his account.

A righteous teacher imitates Christ and is obedient to the Word. A righteous teacher is compassionate as Christ was compassionate. He is honest and transparent as Christ was honest. He is gentle, even as Christ of whom it was said, "A bruised reed shall he not break, and smoking flax shall he not quench" (Matt. 12:20). Children flocked to Him because there was no fear of what He might say or do.

A righteous teacher produces happy youth because they are not afraid. Students know they will not be rebuked for questions they ask or answers they give. They can tell him their darkest thoughts and know he will still accept them. He is gentle.

A righteous teacher produces happy youth because they are loved. They trust his chastening because he exercises self-control and gentleness even in correcting them. He goes the second mile to help them understand. He is compassionate.

A righteous teacher produces happy youth because they admire his wisdom. He backs up his words with Scripture and quickly admits his mistakes and asks forgiveness. He is honest and humble.

Final thought: A righteous teacher produces a happy class!

Apple 165

PROVERBS 29:11

"A fool uttereth all his mind: but a wise man keepeth it in till afterwards."

Wisdom in Controlling the Tongue

To everything there is a season, and a time to every purpose under the heaven…a time to keep silence, and a time to speak," Solomon writes elsewhere (Eccles. 3:1, 7). The control of the tongue is a test of character and wise timing.

The man who speaks hastily is most often proud and foolish, yet he thinks he is simply honest. He says what's on his mind—nothing is hidden. But actually, it simply proves his lack of wisdom and good sense and the depth of his pride to speak his mind quickly.

Pride speaks quickly because it assumes omniscience. We don't need to think; we intuitively know what is right. Hasty speech does not consider that deceptive hearts control minds.

Conversely, humility prays and thinks before it speaks. It admits that we don't know as we should know. It recognizes the omniscience of God and seeks His mind before addressing the situation.

But is it not dishonest to withhold what we think? We should never speak against our mind. But we don't always have to speak our whole mind. Be careful to speak nothing but the truth, but the whole truth may sometimes be restrained (see 1 Sam. 16:1–2).

Final thought: Think and pray before you speak. Speak only what is necessary.

PROVERBS 29:15

"The rod and reproof give wisdom: but a child left to himself bringeth his mother to shame."

Wisdom in Instructive Discipline

The rod without reproof hardens the heart. Reproof without the rod hardens the will. Yet when combined, they soften both the heart and the will.

Eli gave the reproof but spared the rod (1 Sam. 2:22–25; 3:13). The result: two sons with hardened wills and ultimately untimely deaths. The child who gets his own way without restraint becomes an ill–functioning adult. The temper that was thought to be so cute as a child will harden and strengthen in the adult.

Others use the rod but spare the reproof. They are quick to give demerits. They are quick to suspend or expel. Yet they fail to lead the student carefully verse by verse through a discussion of his sin.

Reproof takes time. Impatient teachers often rush through the counseling process allowing little time for growth. The goal is immediate conformity or "You're out of here, buddy!" But growth is a slow process requiring someone who cares enough to correct with the Word and wait for the results. We often have discipline committees, but seldom do we have counseling committees. We would rather use the immediacy of the rod than the time consuming commitment of reproof. The rod requires little effort, time, or thought, but reproof requires all three.

Final thought: Do you take the easy way out and give demerits more freely than counsel? The child without both will bring his school to shame.

Apple 167

PROVERBS 29:15

"The rod and reproof give wisdom: but a child left to himself bringeth his mother to shame."

Wisdom in Giving Reproof

It is not enough to discipline children. We must also disciple them. Discipleship certainly includes the discipline, but it must also include reproof or biblical admonition. Lou Priolo, in his excellent book, *Teach Them Diligently,* asks six probing questions concerning the extent to which parents minister the Word to their children. We would do well to ask the same of teachers, for parents have given them to us to reinforce what they do at home.

1. How well do you know the Scriptures yourself?

2. How often do you refer to the Bible in the course of normal conversation with your children?

3. How adept are you at teaching and relating the Scriptures to them in everyday life?

4. How effectively do you use the Scriptures to reprove (convict) them of their sin? Do you reprove in such a way that causes them to revere God's Word or to disdain it?

5. How consistently do you use the Bible when you correct them?

6. How do you use the Bible to train your children in righteousness to help them to do better in the future?

Final thought: It is our joy both to know and to use the Scriptures as God intended. Scripture alone is sufficient for the life and godliness of our students (2 Pet. 1:3).

"Where there is no vision, the people perish: but he that keepeth the law, happy is he."

Wisdom in Using the Word

This verse is among the most misunderstood verses in Scripture. Missionaries often use it to remind us that we need a vision for missions, or the lost will perish. While we do need a vision for the lost, that is not the teaching of this verse! The *vision* spoken of here is specifically *the revealed Word of God*. When God gave the Old Testament, He did so by visions, dreams, and specific revelation. As long as God communicated His inspired Word to prophets, the people had hope. God was still speaking, giving visions, and imploring the people to repentance. But when God grew silent and no more visions were given to prophets, the people were doomed.

By application, when the Word is preached and teachers counsel students with the Scriptures, the students have hope. But when teachers fail to use the Word and instead rely on medication, on rules, or on demerit systems and handbooks, the students will perish.

We must come to grips with the sufficiency and supremacy of the Word in dealing with students' hearts. Handbooks and rules may temporarily change behavior, but they are impotent to change the heart. Only the revealed Word can reprove, correct, and instruct the heart in righteous living. Do you counsel your students with specific verses of Scripture, or do you correct with the rule book?

Final thought: The power to change a life is in the Word, not the student handbook.

Apple 169

PROVERBS 29:26

"Many seek the ruler's favor; but every man's judgment cometh from the Lord."

Wisdom in Pleasing Him

Seek for God to be your friend. His favor is for a lifetime (see Ps. 30:5, where *life* has the meaning of a lifetime). Sadly, we seek the favor of friends and authorities, ("Many seek the ruler's favor") yet neglect the favor of the only One "with whom we have to do" (Heb. 4:13)!

It is God alone who will ultimately judge us. "But every man's judgment cometh from the Lord." Should we not seek to please Him above all others? Do we not ultimately work for Him? Will the ultimate reward not be handed out at His throne? If only we would go to class each day with eternity's values in view! Our goal should not be to teach or even to change lives. Our ultimate goal should be to please our Heavenly Employer, not our earthly employer!

How do we please the ultimate Judge of all the earth? Not by teaching alone. Teaching alone does not please Him. With what is He pleased? He is pleased when…

- our hearts are filled with Him (Ps. 1:1–2)
- our life is godly (Ps. 51:19)
- we fear Him (Ps. 112:1; 128:1)
- we hear Him; we daily watch at His gates and wait at His doors (Prov. 8:34)

Final thought: Cultivate friendship with God above pleasing man. He is the ultimate rewarder of those that please Him.

PROVERBS 30:5-6

"Every word of God is pure: he is a shield unto them that put their trust in him. Add thou not unto his words lest he reprove thee, and thou be found a liar."

Wisdom in Using God's Word

God's Word is pure. It has stood the trial, and no dross has been found in it. Critics, scholars, nations, and time each added fuel to the fires of testing. Though they sought to find the dross, they found only that God's Word is without error. But, if every word of God is tested and proven true, we must put our total *trust in Him.* "All scripture is…profitable for doctrine, for reproof, for correction, for instruction in righteousness (2 Tim. 3:16), that the man of God may be perfect, thoroughly furnished unto all good works" (v. 17).

Do we truly believe that God's Word is all we need to produce godly youth? Or do we add to His words? Sadly, some seek to manipulate students or to enforce godliness by rules. Rules are not wrong. In fact, they are necessary, but they have nothing to do with producing godliness. Still others accept the theories of clinical psychologists that problems are due to chemical imbalances or emotional scars that must be cured by medication. Yet these theories and mental diseases or disorders have never been medically proven. Sadly, we leave the Bible on the shelf and go to the medicine cabinet or the rule book to correct today's youth!

Final thought: God's Word is sufficient for "all things that pertain unto life and godliness through the knowledge of Him" (2 Pet. 1:3). Use it!

Apple 171

PROVERBS 31:10-12

"Who can find a virtuous woman? For her price is far above rubies. The heart of her husband doth safely trust in her, so that he shall have no need of spoil. She will do him good and not evil all the days of her life."

Virtuous Teachers Are Faithful

The last ten apples in our barrel deal with a virtuous teacher. We will use the passage on the virtuous woman in Proverbs 31 as our text. Though this passage describes the godly wife, we beg permission to apply it to teachers. Should we not all have these qualities? Are they reserved only for moms? Virtuous teachers will have these same qualities.

This passage is an elegant poem of twenty-two verses, with each verse beginning with one of the successive letters of the Hebrew alphabet. So rare is the virtuous woman that the poem begins with the challenge, "Who can find a virtuous woman"? So it may be said of teachers. Where are our virtuous teachers? Is not their price far above rubies?

The first characteristic is faithfulness. Those around her trust her, and know that she will do them good. Her husband is at ease while he is gone. His comfort and success is her highest happiness. The same may be said of the virtuous teacher; both students and parents trust her heart. Parents know that this teacher's greatest burden is the welfare of their child—she will as faithfully care for their children as the parents!

Final thought: A faithful teacher works tirelessly to one end—to see her students mature in the Lord.

PROVERBS 31:13

"She seeketh wool, and flax, and worketh willingly with her hands."

Virtuous Teachers Are Industrious

Throughout this passage the energy and work ethic of the virtuous woman is evident. Manual labor, menial service, and self-denial characterize the virtuous. So it is with virtuous teachers.

Each day we work with the fabric of student lives. We assist their parents in weaving a life that will in the end reflect the glory of God. There is no time for laziness. Every day is an opportunity. We will only have them 180 days, and then they will move on in life. As the virtuous woman *seeketh wool and flax,* so must we seek to bring just the right touch to each life. Some need one cloth, some another. Some need the harsh shades of correction and discipline; some need the pastels of a softer, kinder word. But each requires *work*. A teacher can ill–afford to let students sit day after day and not progress academically and spiritually. She must not trivialize the students' failures, faults, sins, and talents. Each must be energetically *worked* with her hands.

There is no place for laziness in God's business. Paul commands us to be "Not slothful in business; fervent in spirit; serving the Lord" (Rom. 12:11). The last phrase is the key to industry—we serve the Lord. Our love for Him should drive us even more than our love for students. He is too precious to waste a day. His work is the greatest work. We are about the Father's business!

Final thought: Flaming hearts for God produce unflagging hands for others.

Apple 173

PROVERBS 31:14

"She is like the merchants' ships; she bringeth her food from afar."

Virtuous Teachers Are Resourceful

A virtuous wife is resourceful. She does whatever is necessary to provide for the needs of those she loves. As merchant ships bring goods from afar, so she constantly searches for provisions for her family.

A virtuous teacher has these same qualities. He looks for ways to meet the needs of his students. One lady teacher read *Sports Illustrated* for examples and illustrations to which the boys in the class could relate. Another collected huge leaves while sightseeing in Oregon to teach the lesson on leaves from this devotional. The world around us is a treasury of teacher aids.

The resourcefulness of the virtuous wife is driven by her relationship with the Lord (v. 30). The same is true of the virtuous teacher. The more he fears the Lord by seeing Him in everything he reads or sees, the more resources he finds for teaching. David speaks of God *enlarging his heart* (Ps. 119:32), that is, giving him a greater capacity to see and know the Lord. Our hearts and minds are like ships. They must be enlarged with wisdom gathered from the shores of meditation and prayer. The greater our capacity to see the Lord in the world around us and in his Word, the easier it is to return with *ships* (hearts) laden with treasure to bestow on our class.

Final thought: The virtuous teacher enlarges his heart to see the wonders of God in the world and in the Word and brings those resources daily to his class.

PROVERBS 31:15

"She riseth also while it is yet night, and giveth meat to her household, and a portion to her maidens."

Virtuous Teachers Are Disciplined

Virtuous wives are disciplined. They are not only careful to seek what is best, but they also discipline themselves to meet the needs of their family before daybreak. Old Testament wives did not have electricity. What they accomplished was done in the precious hours of daylight. Thus, they rose before sunup to feed their families and maids and gave them their assignments. Then they could give the daylight hours to work in the fields.

Does this not parallel the virtuous teacher? She rises earlier than others so that she might spend time with the Lord before her family wakes. She knows that her own heart must be fed and her mind given proper instructions from the Lord. The time she will have with her students will not allow her the luxury of time with the Lord. Thus, she must prepare food while it is still night. Then she will have something with which to feed her class during the day!

Such a life requires discipline. Susanna Wesley (who had 22 children) arose at 4 a.m. to spend an hour or more with the Lord before her children awoke. Such discipline was rewarded with godly children, two of which, John and Charles, still impact the world (two hundred years later) through their songs and writings.

Final thought: What we do before school may be more important than what we do in school!

Apple 175

PROVERBS 31:16

"She considereth a field, and buyeth it: with the fruit of her hands she planteth a vineyard."

Virtuous Teachers Are Cultivators

The virtuous woman is an astute real estate appraiser! She carefully studies property and wisely chooses the field she thinks is best for a vineyard. After making her decision, she purchases the field and just as carefully works the field with her own hands to insure a rich harvest.

Likewise, the goal of a virtuous teacher is to produce a crop of mature, godly youth. But such a goal is only realized through hours of toil and care. First, the virtuous teacher considers the field (in this case, the hearts of her students). She studies their families, their school records, their likes, dislikes, aptitudes, and weaknesses. She would sow on fertile ground. Each *field* is different. She will not work by impulse but by purpose. She *considers* each field. She looks at the soil of the heart so she can be most effective in each life. One likes sports, so she will use sports terminology; another has trouble comprehending text, so she will draw pictures and diagrams; a third child is starved for affection, so she will give him special attention. She *considers* each child.

Virtuous teachers also *plant* with their *hands.* They are personally involved in the life of each child. They cheer for them, counsel with them, eat lunch with them, and play with them on the playground. My favorite teacher (my virtuous wife) challenges her 6th grade boys in one–on–one basketball so she can better reach their hearts!

Final thought: Those who cultivate hearts produce a rich harvest.

Virtuous Teachers Stay in Shape

A virtuous wife is concerned for her health. Her family needs her. She exercises. She is careful of her weight and her stamina. She is not motivated by vanity but because she knows that her health is vital to the welfare of her home. Her children need her energy. Her husband needs her vitality. When Mom is sick, so is the whole household!

The virtuous teacher should be so concerned with his health. He believes so strongly in the value of his labor that he diligently *strengthens* himself for the task. When the health is gone, the opportunity for service is gone! When the energy is gone, the vineyard dries. He must be strong to work in the field each day.

Paul speaks of two types of health: physical and spiritual (1 Tim. 4:8; 3 John 2). Though godly health is paramount, physical well-being is necessary. Both must be nurtured so that the servant of God might be better able to serve.

Godly exercise includes daily meditation on God in the Word, prayer, Bible study, witnessing, and faithfully serving those students God brings into your life.

Physical exercise is also vital. A virtuous teacher will not be slovenly in *girding his loins with strength*. He will watch his weight and keep himself fit—for the sake of his Lord. Both his spiritual and physical regimen are designed to serve the Lord better.

Final thought: An unfit teacher is unfit to teach!

Apple 177

PROVERBS 31:19-20

"She layeth her hands to the spindle, and her hands hold the distaff. She stretcheth out her hand to the poor; yea, she reacheth forth her hands to the needy."

Virtuous Teachers Are Energetically Compassionate

These two verses seem to address two different subjects (industry in v. 19 and compassion in v. 20). Yet they are linked by four parallel phrases "she layeth her hands" (v. 19) with "she stretcheth out her hand" (v. 20); and "her hands hold" (v. 19) with "she reacheth forth her hands" (v. 20). This structure reveals the close connection between industry and compassion. Only the compassionate have the energy to give themselves for others! Laziness seldom shows kindness or concern. While laziness dulls the mind and drains energy, love sharpens both.

Love energized the virtuous woman. She spent long hours at the loom making garments for them. Likewise, the teacher who loves her class stretches out her hand to the poor and lays her hands to the distaff. Compassionate teachers work tirelessly for their students. Compassion motivates teachers to help needy students. Compassion thinks of ways to make a subject more understandable. Compassion creates new ideas to help a slow student learn. Compassion meets with parents, prays with children, spends extra time with struggling youth, draws pictures to help visual learners grasp concepts, and doesn't quit because she is tired. Compassion never stops or quits. Her palms, though tired, still grasp the distaff.

Final thought: Love energizes and tirelessly sacrifices to reach every student.

PROVERBS 31:21

"She is not afraid of the snow for her household: for all her household are clothed with scarlet."

Virtuous Teachers Prepare Students for Winter

Your students must be prepared for a dangerous future! Sin and temptation—disguised to deceive—wait around the corner. Divorce, immorality, a cut-throat business world, terrorism, liberal theology, moral relativism, and a world gone mad seek to pull youth into their devouring vortex. Only the most careful teacher can say with confidence, "I am not afraid for my students because I have given them all they need for the snow of life."

As the virtuous woman prepared her children for the harsh realities of winter, so the virtuous teacher must prepare his students for the harsh realities they face. He realizes that sin lies in each student's heart and seeks to wash it white as snow with the scarlet blood of Christ. Further, he knows that even saved youth struggle with the flesh. Anger, bitterness, pride, greed, an unforgiving spirit, and a myriad of other sins lie as sleeping beasts in the heart of each child. Students must learn how to biblically deal with each. Virtuous teachers show them how, even while teaching history or literature. They challenge students to analyze each piece of literature in light of what the Bible teaches. They are taught the consequences of pride, greed, immorality, and anger in history and are shown how leaders and nations could have biblically dealt with their own sinfulness. To teach history otherwise is to fail to give your students scarlet garments for the winter.

Final thought: Virtuous teachers do more than teach materials. They prepare students to overcome the beasts crouching in their own hearts.

Apple 179

PROVERBS 31:22–23

"She maketh herself coverings of tapestry; her clothing is silk and purple. Her husband is known in the gates, when he sitteth among the elders of the land."

Virtuous Teachers Are Attractive

The virtuous woman is concerned with her appearance because it is a reflection of her husband. Silk and purple indicated dignity and honor for her husband, who held a place of prominence in the community. To be unkempt or slovenly would disgrace her earthly lord—a thing she was loath to do.

Likewise, the virtuous teacher would dress to honor his Lord. A disheveled or sloppy appearance reflects a careless concern for God's glory. Though Scripture reminds us that God looks on the heart, it also reveals that God is concerned with our appearance! Though He may not care about our physical looks, He is interested in our attire! Modesty, cleanliness, order, and appropriateness of dress are principles God lays down in His Word.

The teacher who comes to work with stained or wrinkled clothing disgraces the purity and holiness of His Lord! The teacher who is sloppy and disorderly in dress detracts from the orderliness of God. When we represent the King of Kings, we should dress accordingly. Teens may be turned off by an unkempt appearance or yesterday's breakfast on our tie! "Whether therefore ye eat, or drink, or whatsoever ye do, do all to the glory of God" (1 Cor. 10:31).

Final thought: You represent the King of Kings. Dress accordingly.

"Her children arise up, and call her blessed; her husband also, and he praiseth her."

Virtuous Teachers Are Blessed

So wise and godly is the virtuous woman that both her children and her husband honor and praise her. The sacrifice is rewarded. The burning of midnight oil, the candle that does not go out by night, and the selfless life produce grateful children and a thankful husband.

The virtuous teacher is also blessed. Her blessings are not measured in dollars and cents but in something far more valuable—in lives that are forever changed and in a Lord who is well pleased! Paul said, "For what is our hope, or joy, or crown of rejoicing? Are not even ye in the presence of our Lord Jesus Christ at his coming?" (1 Thess. 2:19). Is this not our joy as well?

I praise a second grade teacher, Mrs. Thelma Boyd. I don't remember the material she taught, but I remember she sent me a birthday card every year until I was married! I recall my third grade teacher, Mrs. Nora Shelton, who hugged me and loved me and let me stay at her house while Mom and Dad were on an extended trip. I well recall my fifth grade teacher, Mrs. Hubbard, who taught me that short people were special! Finally, I am indebted to Lincoln Napoleon Donevant who taught me to think and to discipline my life. These teachers will always be a part of my ministry and my life, not because of the material they taught but because of the lives they lived!

Final thought: How will you be remembered: as someone who taught, or as someone who cared?

APPENDIX

The Value of Wisdom

1:8–9	An ornament of grace unto thy head and chains about thy neck
1:33	Safety, peace, and fearlessness
2:1–8	Wisdom, knowledge, understanding, the fear of the Lord, and preservation
2:10–12	Discretion, preservation, protection, and deliverance from evil people
3:2	Long life (3:18; 4:10)
3:4	Favor with God and men
3:6	Divine guidance
3:8	Health (4:22)
3:10	Material blessing
3:13	Happiness
3:14	More valuable than silver and gold
3:15	More precious than rubies and all you may want in life
3:16	Long life, riches, and honor
3:17	Pleasantness and peace
3:22	Life to your soul and grace to your neck
3:23	Safety and sure–footedness
3:24	Lack of fear and sweet sleep
3:26	Confidence
3:33	Your house will be blessed
3:34	Grace in time of need
3:35	Glory (4:9)
4:6	Preservation and protection (6:22)
4:8	Promotion
8:11	Better than rubies
8:18	The way to riches and honor
8:19	Better than gold and silver
8:35	Brings favor from the Lord

The Curse of Disobedience

1:10–19	Vanity and loss of the life
1:26–28	Calamity (while God laughs), fear, destruction, distress, anguish, and unanswered prayer
2:18	Death
3:33	Your house will be cursed
3:35	Shame
5:22	He will be taken with his own wickedness
6:11	Poverty (6:26)
6:15	Calamity
6:32	Destruction of his own soul
6:33	Wounds, dishonour, and reproach

By the way did you know?

We also have a God–focused school curriculum
to help you reach your students' hearts.

Teaching Bible is not like teaching other subjects. Bible classes must not only teach Bible content, but also lead young people to know God and draw near to Him in a special, saving relationship. God works to change us spiritually from the inside out. If you want your Bible classes to have lasting impact in your students' lives, you must teach Bible with these truths in mind. Positive Action Bible Curriculum is designed to help your teachers and students approach their study of God's Word in this way.

Curriculum distinctives:

1. Leads young people to know God through His Word
2. Teaches young people to apply biblical wisdom to specific life situations
3. Establishes the priority of internal heart transformation over external reform
4. Focuses on developing inner character
5. Recognizes various levels of thinking skills

**For more information or to receive a catalog, please visit us at
www.positiveaction.org or call (800) 688–3008.**